Merry Christmas Inara

From Nathanaël and
Nicolaas

Dec. 1998

The OXFORD Children's A to Z of Mathematics

David Glover

OXFORD UNIVERSITY PRESS

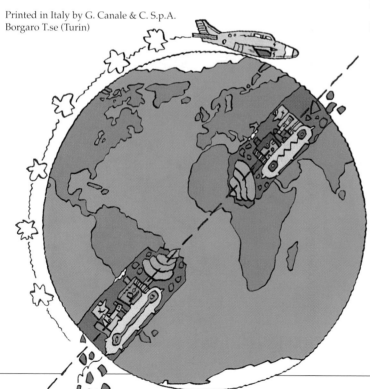

Acknowledgements

Design: Christopher Howson

Picture Research: Image Select International

Abbreviations: t = top; b = bottom; l = left;
r = right; c = centre; back = background

Photographs

The publishers would like to thank the following for
permission to reproduce the following photographs:

Allsport: 5b/Pascal Rondeau, 19/Howard Boylan,
44b/David Cannon, 44/45t

Ancient Art and Architecture: 27 back, 54
© 1995 M.C. Escher/**Cordon Art**-Baarn-Holland. All
rights reserved: 60

Julian Cotton Photo Library: 41(both)/Jason Hawkes,
Aerial Collection

Christopher Howson: 48

Images Colour Library: 9/Charles Walker, 14, 18, 28, 32–33 back
33l, 38, 38–39 back

Image Select: 42, 56/NASA

Jacana: 5r/Alain Le Touquin, 46b/Robert Bousquet

Planet Earth Picture Library: 57/Peter Palmer, 58t,c/Alan Baines

Ann Ronan/Image Select: 8–9, 24, 25(both), 49

Science Photo Library: 11/Adrienne Hart-Davis, 12(both)/Dale
Boyer/NASA, 15/Hasler & Pierce/NASA GSFC, 23t/Alfred Pasieka,
33r/Hank Morgan, 41t/Dr Gary Settles

Peter Smith: 63

Martin Soukias: 20, 21, 32, 36, 51, 55 both, 58b, 61 all

Spectrum: 7/E J King, 34–35

Telegraph Colour Library: 22–23b, 53/Ted Kurihara

Illustrations and diagrams

Christopher Howson: 4lc, 5c, 7ct and cb, 19tc, 20bl, 26tr, 31tl,
34, 35t, 40tl, 51cr, 53bl, 59tl;

Andrea Norton: 4tl, 6cr and b, 12–13b, 14cr, 15cl, 17b, 18br,
21b, 22tr, 24tl and b, 26bl, 29b, 32l, 34tl, 36t, 37br, 38cl
39lc, 40tc, 42tr, 43tl, 44tl, 47cr and br, 50br, 51tl and b
52tl and br, 59bl, 60cr;

Lesley Saddington: 4-5c, 4br, 6tl and lc and bc, 7l, 8bl,
9br, 11tr, 16tr, 18–19c, 19bl, 22bl, 27cr and b, 28b, 29c
31b, 34c, 35cr, 36br, 38–39b, 40bl, 42br, 48tr and br,
49c, 50tl and tr and bl, 52bl, 53t, 54, 56tr and cr and
br, 58tl and cl, 60l, 61cr, 62bl, 63tr and bl;

Martin Sanders: 17t, 28t;

Chris Winn: front cover tl and c, 7tc, 8lc and tr, 10c, 55tl
and tr and br;

Tony Wells: front cover tr and b, back cover tl, tr and c,
10tl, 11cl, 14bl, 16lc and br, 19tl, 20lc, 21, 23br, 25c,
26br, 30t and b, 33br, 37cl, 38c, 40cr, 43b, 45b, 46br,
47lc, 48lc, 52cr, 57cl, 59br, 60bl, 61br, 64c

Dear Reader

Love it or hate it, mathematics is everywhere. It's not just at school where you have to do sums, work out angles, follow plans and understand graphs. You use mathematics all the time: playing a computer game, shopping, baking a cake, reading a bus timetable, building a model aeroplane – things that everyone can do, and yet they all need just as much mathematics as your school homework.

The *A to Z of Mathematics* explains 300 mathematical words, using everyday examples that make them easy to understand. Once you know that an 'integer' is another name for a whole number or that a 'function' is just a rule for changing one number into another, then mathematics starts to make sense!

As you explore this A to Z you will discover that mathematics is fascinating and fun – do you know how to make a strip of paper with only one side, why computer errors are called bugs or why there were riots in London when a new calendar was introduced in 1752? Read on . . .

David Glover

A

abacus

An abacus is a simple calculating machine. It uses stones, beads or rings as counters. A Chinese abacus has sets of wooden rings which slide along rods. You can add and subtract numbers with an abacus by moving the rings.

A Chinese shopkeeper adds up with an abacus. ▷

acute angle

An acute angle is an angle which is smaller than a **right angle**. See also **angle**.

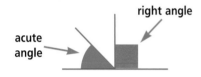

right angle

acute angle

addition

Addition is finding the **total** of two or more numbers. The plus sign (+) in an addition sum shows that numbers are being added together.

If you add three bricks to a pile of five bricks you will have a total of eight bricks:
5 + 3 = 8
If you add another two bricks the total is ten:
8 + 2 = 10
You could do the addition in one sum:
5 + 3 + 2 = 10

You probably did your first addition sums by 'counting on'. If you start with the number five and count on by three, you get the answer eight. In the end you just know that five plus three is eight, without thinking. Everyone still counts on occasionally, just to be sure!

algebra

Algebra is a kind of language or code for mathematics. Mathematicians use algebra to solve problems and to investigate number patterns. In algebra letters are used to stand for numbers. For example, the letter x is often used to stand for a number we do not know and want to find out.

The distance between any two posts in a fence is 5 metres (m). What is the distance between four posts? Let's say that the distance is x. We can see that there are three spaces between the four posts. This means that $x = 3 \times 5$ m, so $x = 15$ m.

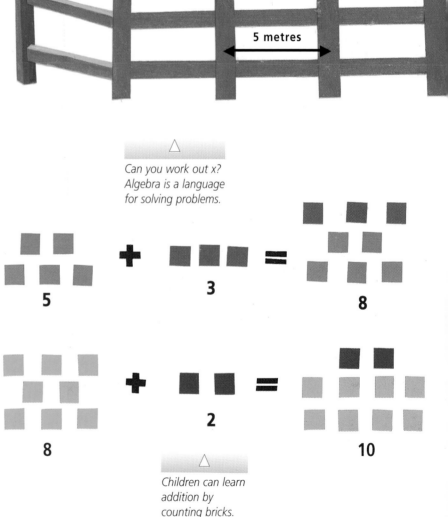

x metres

5 metres

Can you work out x? Algebra is a language for solving problems.

5

+

3

=

8

8

+

2

=

10

Children can learn addition by counting bricks.

When you solve a problem using algebra, you can discover number patterns. These number patterns are shown by an **equation**.

Can you find the distance between any number of posts in the fence?

If you work out the answer for different numbers of posts, say 3, 5 or 6, you will find there is a pattern. The number of spaces between the posts is always one less than the number of posts. This means that x (the distance between any number of posts) can be found with an equation:
$x = $ (number of posts $-$ 1) $\times$ 5.

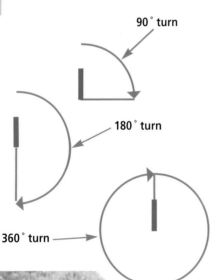

angle

An angle is the amount by which something turns or 'rotates'. Angles are measured in **degrees**. The symbol for degrees is $^{\circ}$. There are 360° in a circle. If you turn all the way around then you have turned through 360 degrees. Half a turn is 180 degrees (180°). A quarter turn is 90 degrees (90°) which is also called a **right angle**. See also **rotation**.

90° turn

180° turn

360° turn

anticlockwise

When something goes round anticlockwise it goes round in the opposite direction to the hands on a clock.

approximate

An approximate answer is very close to the right answer but it may not be exactly the same. For example, your age might be nine years, three months and two days. If someone asks you 'How old are you?', you usually reply with the approximate answer 'nine'.

Nine and a quarter is approximately equal to nine.

The arc of a rainbow is part of a circle.

arc

An arc is a curved line that would make a complete **circle** if you continued it. A rainbow is an arc of colour in the sky. Completely circular rainbows are sometimes seen from high-flying aircraft. You can use a pair of **compasses** to draw an arc.

Archimedes

See **famous mathematicians**.

This water skier is leaning over by an angle of nearly 90°.

area

Area is a measure of the total **surface** of a shape or object. You can find the area of a **square** or a **rectangle** by multiplying its length by its width.

area = length x width

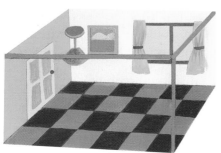

A room which is 6 metres (m) long and 4 m wide has a floor area of 24 (6 x 4) square metres (m²).

It is more difficult to find out the area of an irregular shape such as a leaf. One way is to divide it into a lot of small squares. Each square could be, say, 1 centimetre (cm) long and 1 cm wide.

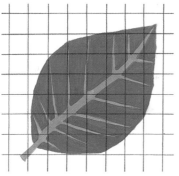

Find the area of the leaf by counting the whole squares and the part squares that are bigger than half a square. (The answer is at the bottom of the page.)

arithmetic

In arithmetic you add, subtract, **multiply** and **divide** numbers. You use arithmetic to find the answers to problems and **sums**.
See also **addition, subtraction**.

average

The average of a group of numbers is a typical or middle value. The average height of 10-year-old boys is 1.35 metres (m). The average temperature in Sydney, Australia, in January is 25 degrees Celsius (°C).

You find the average of a set of numbers by adding them and dividing the total by how many numbers there are. This average is called the **mean**.
See also **median, mode**.

To work out the average number of peas in five pods, find the total number of peas:
6 + 5 + 8 + 3 + 8 = 30.
Divide 30 by 5 (the number of pods):
30 ÷ 5 = 6.
The average number of peas is six, although some pods have more peas than the average and some have fewer.

The red line shows the average height of the five children.

average height

height in metres

axis

An axis is an imaginary line through the middle of any solid shape.

An axis is also one of the **horizontal** or **vertical** lines on a **graph**. The axes (plural of axis) are used to measure the position of points on the graph.

axis

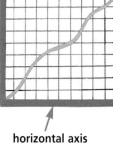

A cylindrical grass roller turns smoothly around its axis.

vertical axis

horizontal axis

ANSWER: 33 square centimetres (cm²)

B

bar chart

A bar chart is a diagram with a row of **vertical** or **horizontal** bars. The length of each bar shows an amount of something.

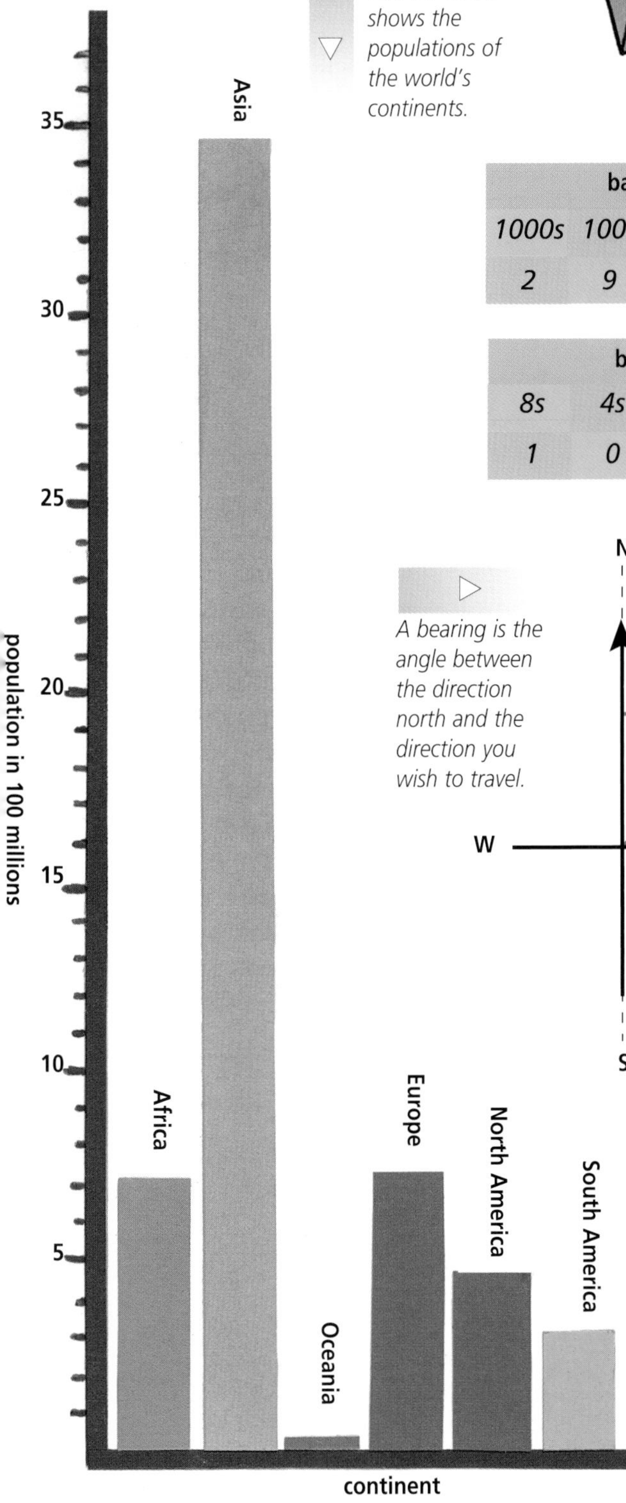

This bar chart shows the populations of the world's continents.

population in 100 millions

35 — Asia

30 —

25 —

20 —

15 —

10 — Africa · Europe · North America · South America

5 — Oceania

continent

base

The base of a shape or an object is the bottom edge or surface on which it rests.

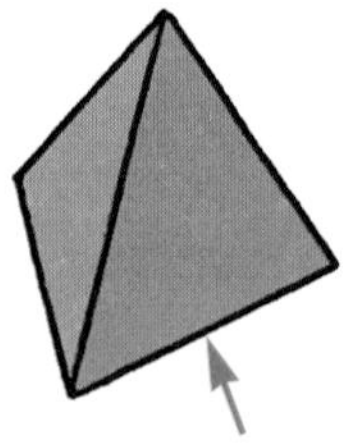

base

The base of a number is the number of units that we use for counting. We normally count units from 0 to 9 and then write 10, to show one ten and no units. This is called base ten. Computers use base two. In base two, 10 means one two and no units.

base 10			
1000s	*100s*	*10s*	*1s*
2	*9*	*4*	*5*

base 2			
8s	*4s*	*2s*	*1s*
1	*0*	*1*	*1*

In base 10, the number 2945 means two thousands, nine hundreds, four tens and five units.

In base 2, the number 1011 means one eight, no four, one two and one one. This is equal to 11 (8 + 2 + 1 = 11) in base 10.

See also **binary number, decimal number.**

A bearing is the angle between the direction north and the direction you wish to travel.

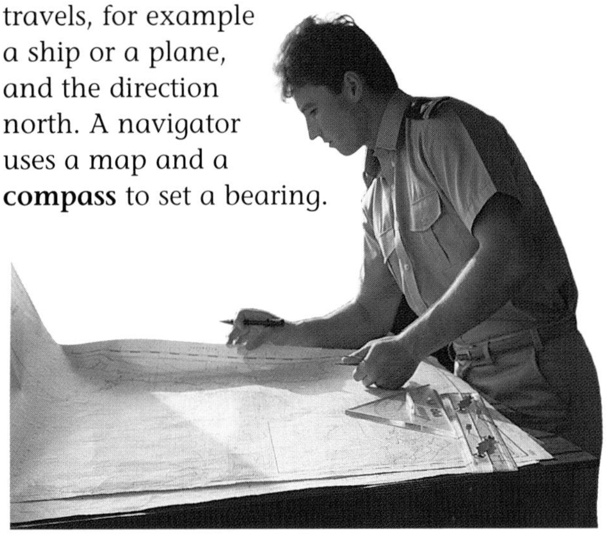

N

60°

W — E

S

A ship's navigator checks a bearing on a map.

bearing

A bearing is the angle between the direction in which something travels, for example a ship or a plane, and the direction north. A navigator uses a map and a **compass** to set a bearing.

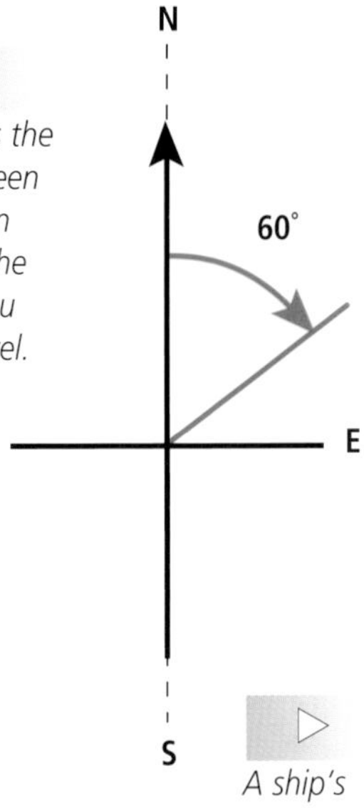

billion

A billion is one thousand million. It is written 1 000 000 000. In the UK a billion used to be one million million (1 000 000 000 000) but this meaning is no longer in common use.

binary number

Binary numbers only contain the **digits** 0 and 1. Normally we use **decimal numbers** with ten digits, from 0 to 9. We count these digits in units, tens, hundreds, thousands, etc. The decimal number 101 means one hundred, no tens and one unit. Binary numbers are counted in units, twos, fours, eights, sixteens and so on. The binary number 101 means one four, no two and one unit.

Computers work with binary numbers because switches or lights can be used to stand for the digits 1 (on) and 0 (off).
See also **base**, **computer**.

These lights are showing the binary number 101101. This is equal to the decimal number 45 as 32 + 0 + 8 + 4 + 0 + 1 = 45.

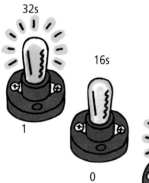
32s
1

16s
0

8s
1

4s
1

2s
0

1s
1

block graph

A block graph is a special kind of **graph**. It has stacks of blocks to show the number of things in different groups.

Ten children were asked to name their favourite colour. Their answers are shown on this block graph.

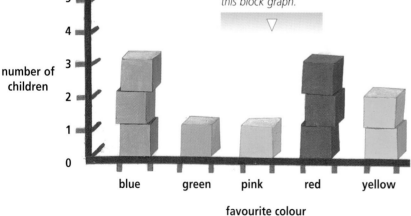

number of children

5
4
3
2
1
0

blue   green   pink   red   yellow

favourite colour

calculator

A calculator is a pocket-sized **computer**. It is specially built to do mathematical calculations. The first electronic calculators were made in the 1970s. They were the same size as a briefcase and they cost thousands of pounds each.
See also **computer**.

Nowadays you can buy a calculator the size of a credit card for less than £10.

calendar

A calendar is a system for counting the years and dividing the year into months and days. Different calendars are used across the world. Each one counts the years starting from a special event, which is often a religious one.

The Gregorian calendar is used in most western countries. It counts years from the birth of Christ in the year AD 1. (AD stands for *anno domini*, which is Latin for 'in the year of our Lord'.) Each new year starts on the first day of January, and there are twelve months in the year.

When the Gregorian calendar was introduced in England in 1752 to replace the old Julian calendar, the date was changed overnight from 2 September to 14 September. This caused riots in London. People demanded to have the eleven missing days returned. (Imagine if your birthday had been on 4 September!)

The Aztec Sun Stone is an ancient calendar from Mexico. You can see the face of the Aztec sun god, Tonatiuh, in the centre.

The Jewish calendar counts years from the date of the creation given by the Old Testament. According to this calendar AD 1996 is the year 5756. The Islamic calendar counts from the date when the prophet Mohammed fled from Mecca to Medina. There are 354 days in an Islamic year (355 in leap years) and AD 1996 is the year 1417.

A calendar is also a chart on which the days and months of the year are shown.
See also **date**, **time**, **year**.

In the Chinese calendar 1996 is the year of the rat. There are 12 different animal years. It will be the year of the rat again in 2008.

capacity

The capacity of a container is the amount of water or other liquid that it will hold. A five-litre jug holds five litres of liquid. A litre is a measure of **volume**.

cardinal number

See **number**.

Carroll diagram

A Carroll diagram is a way of sorting things into groups, or sets. For example, in a box of shapes some shapes are red, some shapes are cubes, some shapes are red cubes and some are neither red nor cubes. You could use a Carroll diagram to sort these shapes into four sets.

A mathematician called Charles Dodgson invented Carroll diagrams as an alternative to **Venn diagrams**. He is better known as Lewis Carroll, the author of *Alice's Adventures in Wonderland*.
See also **set**.

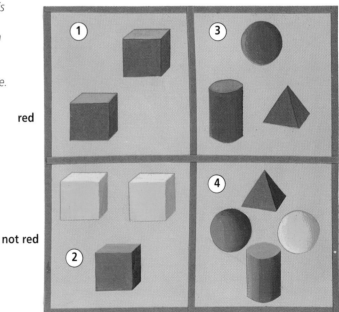

This Carroll diagram has four sets: ① cubes that are red; ② cubes that are not red; ③ shapes that are red but are not cubes; ④ shapes that are not red and not cubes. Where would you place a red cylinder, a yellow sphere and a blue cube? (The answers are at the bottom of the page.)

Celsius

The Celsius scale measures temperature in degrees Celsius, or ˚C for short. It has 100 divisions, or degrees, between the temperature when water freezes and ice melts (0 ˚C), and the temperature of boiling water (100 ˚C).

The Celsius scale used to be known as the centigrade scale (*centi-* means 100). The scale was renamed after the Swedish scientist, Anders Celsius, who invented it in 1742.

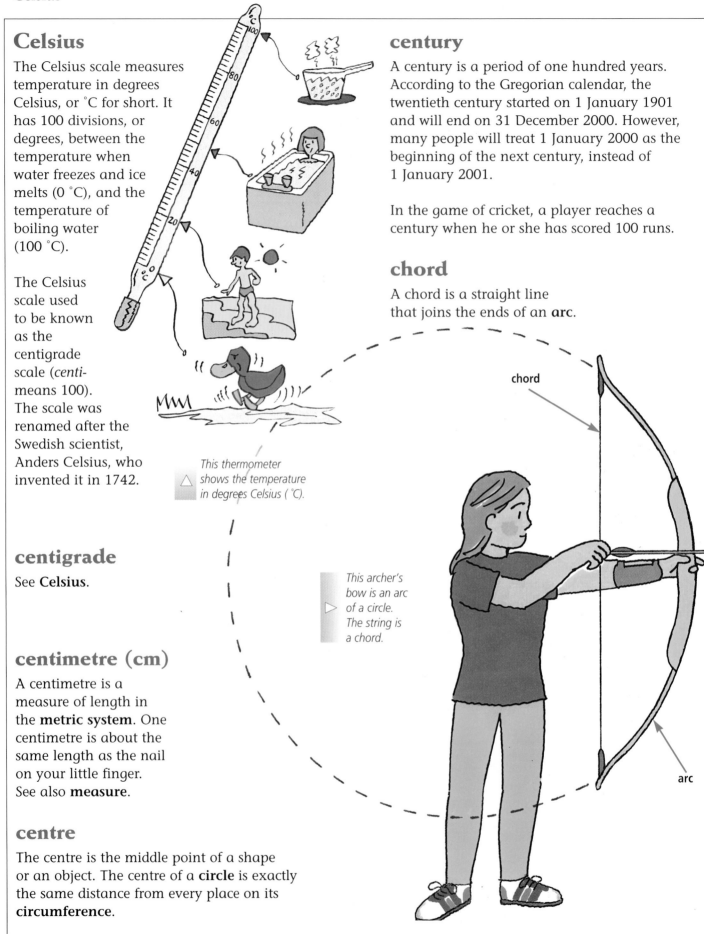

This thermometer shows the temperature in degrees Celsius (˚C).

centigrade

See **Celsius**.

centimetre (cm)

A centimetre is a measure of length in the **metric system**. One centimetre is about the same length as the nail on your little finger. See also **measure**.

centre

The centre is the middle point of a shape or an object. The centre of a **circle** is exactly the same distance from every place on its **circumference**.

century

A century is a period of one hundred years. According to the Gregorian calendar, the twentieth century started on 1 January 1901 and will end on 31 December 2000. However, many people will treat 1 January 2000 as the beginning of the next century, instead of 1 January 2001.

In the game of cricket, a player reaches a century when he or she has scored 100 runs.

chord

A chord is a straight line that joins the ends of an **arc**.

chord

This archer's bow is an arc of a circle. The string is a chord.

arc

circle

A circle is a perfect shape with every place around its edge at exactly the same distance from the centre. The distance from the centre of the circle to the edge is called the **radius**.

circumference

The circumference is the edge of a shape, especially a curved shape such as a circle.

The circumference is also the distance all the way around the edge of a shape. See also **pi**.

coaxial

Two shapes or objects are coaxial if they share an **axis**.

axis

coaxial cylinders

compass

A compass is an instrument for drawing circles and arcs. It has a pair of hinged legs with a sharp point on one leg and a pencil or pen attached to the other. It is sometimes called compasses or a pair of compasses.

A compass is also an instrument for finding the direction north. It has a magnetic needle that always points to the north. You use a compass to set a bearing.

The needle of a magnetic compass points north.

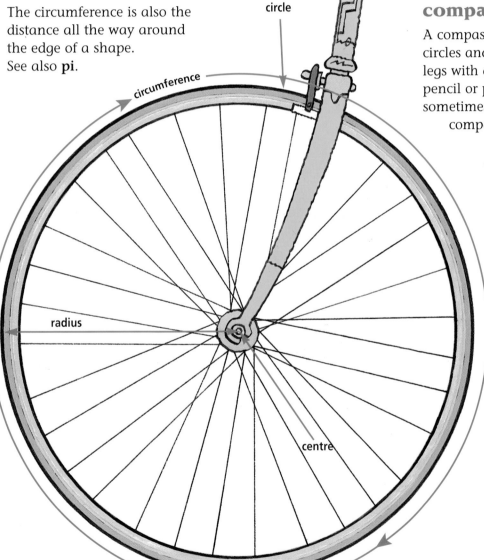

circle

circumference

radius

centre

clockwise

When something goes around clockwise it goes around in the same direction as the hands on a clock.

compass bearing

See **bearing**.

Computer

Computers are found in nearly every part of our lives. We use them to store words, sounds and pictures, to control factory robots, to create television pictures, to add up our shopping bill in the supermarket, to play games, to forecast the weather and to design cars. You probably use a computer at school, and you may have one at home as well.

Computers are all-purpose machines that work by making mathematical calculations. The idea for the first computer came from a mathematician called Charles Babbage (1792–1871). In 1832 he invented a machine called an 'analytical engine'. It could do mathematical calculations by following instructions which were fed into the engine on punched cards. Babbage drew up complex designs for his engines, but they were not built during his lifetime.

Engineers use powerful computers to help design streamlined aircraft.

Everything inside a modern computer works in the binary system. Millions of tiny electronic switches are used to store and make calculations with **binary numbers**.

A single compact disc holds more than 600 million binary numbers.

▷
Modern personal computers can store huge amounts of information and make millions of mathematical calculations in one second.

▷
When you move the computer mouse, an arrow or pointer moves on the screen. You can use the mouse to choose things from the screen by pointing and clicking, or you can use it to draw lines and shapes.

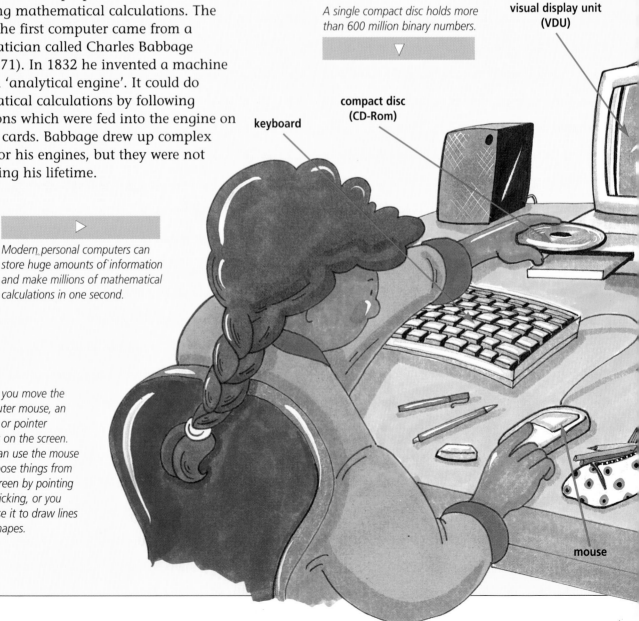

keyboard

compact disc (CD-Rom)

visual display unit (VDU)

mouse

The switches can be either 'ON' or 'OFF'. When a switch is ON, it stands for the binary number 1; when it is OFF it stands for the binary number 0. Every word, sound and picture is just a long list of 1s and 0s. Even the letters of the alphabet are stored as binary numbers in a special code called the ASCII code: A is 1000001, B is 100001, and C is 1000011.

All computers have several basic parts. The processor does calculations and moves numbers. The memory stores both the program (a list of instructions which tells the processor what to do) and the information, or **data**, that the computer is working on. The programs and data

Computers can be linked together to swap information.

that go into the computer are the 'input'. The results that come out are the 'output'.

If you look closely at a picture on a computer screen you can see lots of tiny coloured squares called 'pixels'. The position of each pixel is given by a pair of **coordinates**. Another number gives the colour of each pixel.

One of the first general-purpose electronic computers was built in Manchester, England, in 1948. One day a moth got inside the computer and caused a breakdown. Ever since then, problems with computers have been known as bugs!

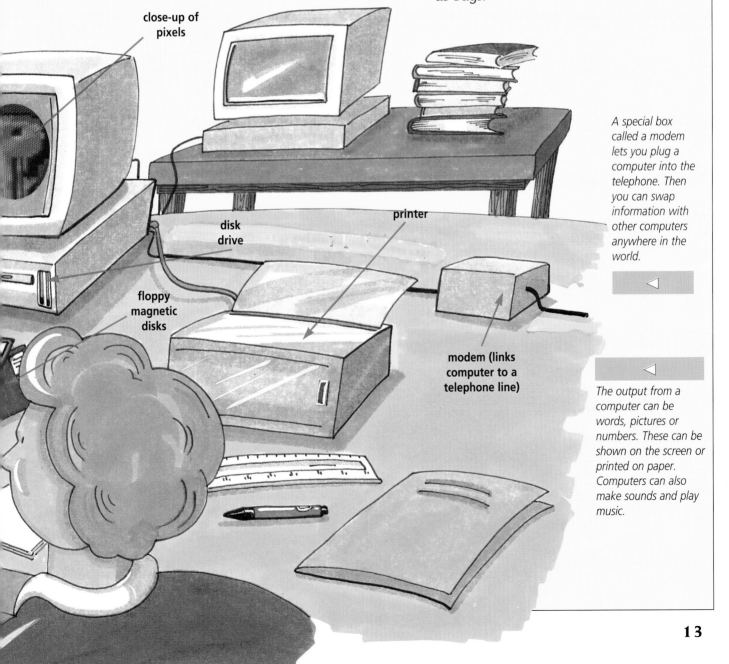

close-up of pixels

disk drive

floppy magnetic disks

printer

modem (links computer to a telephone line)

A special box called a modem lets you plug a computer into the telephone. Then you can swap information with other computers anywhere in the world.

◁

◁

The output from a computer can be words, pictures or numbers. These can be shown on the screen or printed on paper. Computers can also make sounds and play music.

concave

A concave surface curves inwards like the inside of a bowl or a spoon.

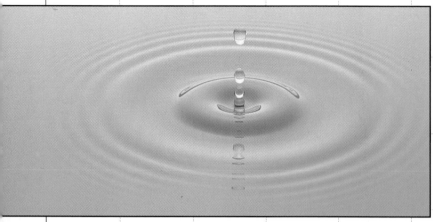

congruent

Two shapes are congruent if they are exactly the same. One shape can be placed exactly on the other. The sides of congruent shapes must be the same length, and the angles at the corners must also be the same.

◁ *These triangles will fit exactly on top of each other. They are congruent.*

concentric

Two shapes are concentric if their centres are at the same point. When you throw a stone into a pond it makes concentric ripples on the water's surface.

The ripples made by this water drip are concentric circles.

cone

A cone is a solid shape with a pointed top and a circular **base**. See also **shape**.

◁ *This wizard's hat is cone-shaped or conical.*

▷ *These triangles are not congruent. They will not fit exactly over each other, however you turn them.*

conservation

Conservation means keeping the same quantity. Which is more: 50 chocolates in a box or 50 chocolates spread out on a plate? They are the same, of course. The number of chocolates does not change when you take them out of the box (unless you eat some!). This is called conservation of number.

When you pour water from a short fat glass into a tall thin one the amount of water does not change. This is called conservation of **volume**.

conversion

Conversion means change. Sometimes you need to change, or convert, a length given in inches into a length in centimetres (cm).

How many centimetres are 12 inches (1 foot)?
There are 2.54 cm in one inch, so 12 inches is
12 × 2.54 = 30.48 cm.
There are 30.48 cm in 12 inches.

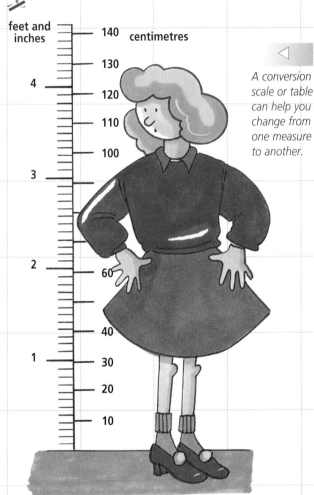

◁ A conversion scale or table can help you change from one measure to another.

We say that 2.54 is the conversion factor for changing inches to centimetres. You may want to convert litres into gallons, dollars into pounds or miles into kilometres. Each pair of measures has its own conversion factor. See also **measure**.

convex

A convex surface curves outwards like the outside of a ball or the back of a spoon.

coordinate

Coordinates are numbers that give the position of a point on a **graph**. The first number, or coordinate, gives the distance along the horizontal **axis**; the second coordinate gives the distance along the vertical axis. You can use the two coordinates to locate the point.

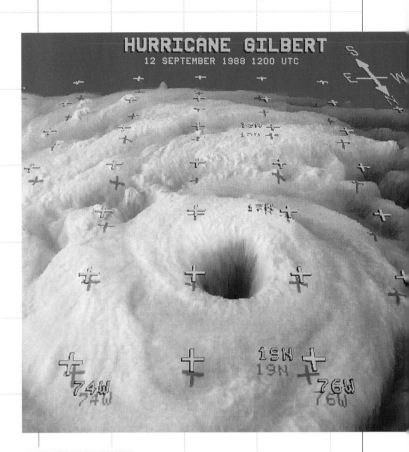

HURRICANE GILBERT
12 SEPTEMBER 1988 1200 UTC

△ Scientists can read the coordinates of the different parts of this hurricane from the grid marked on the satellite image.

△ The coordinates of this point on the grid drawn on this page are 16,2. What are the coordinates of the star on the wizard's hat? (The answer is at the bottom of the page.)

You also use coordinates to find the exact position of a place on a map. Again, the first coordinate gives the distance in the horizontal direction and the second gives the distance in the vertical direction.

Air traffic controllers need three coordinates to find the position of an aircraft: its distance, its **bearing** and its height.

count

When you count you are saying (or thinking) numbers in a certain order: one, two, three, four . . . or two, four, six, eight . . .

When you count objects you find out how many there are by matching each object with a number name.

cross-section

A cross-section is an imaginary slice through a solid shape. In mathematics a cross-section is usually made by cutting the shape at **right angles** to one of its **dimensions**, such as its length or its height.

A cross-section can also mean a drawing of the imaginary slice.

◁

This drawing shows a cross-section through a space shuttle.

cube

A cube is a solid shape with six square faces, such as a dice.

To cube a number means to multiply that number by itself twice. The cube of two, or two cubed, is 2 x 2 x 2, which equals 8. The normal way of showing that a number is cubed is to write a small number 3 just after and above the number: $2^3 = 2 \times 2 \times 2 = 8$.
See also **shape**.

cubic number

When you multiply a whole number by itself twice, the answer is called a cubic number. Cubic numbers greater than one can be arranged as dots in the shape of a cube.

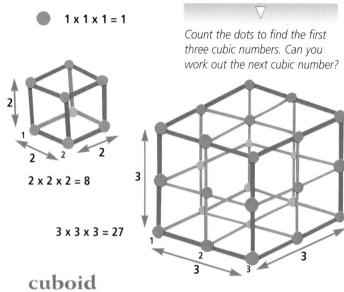

● 1 x 1 x 1 = 1

▽

Count the dots to find the first three cubic numbers. Can you work out the next cubic number?

2 x 2 x 2 = 8

3 x 3 x 3 = 27

cuboid

A cuboid is a solid shape with six rectangular faces, such as a brick.
See also **rectangle, shape**.

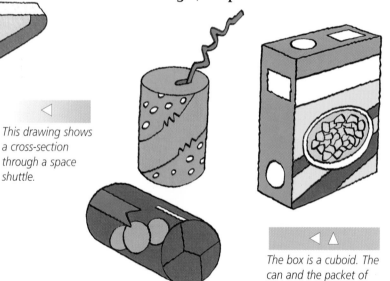

◁ △

The box is a cuboid. The can and the packet of biscuits are cylinders.

cylinder

A cylinder is a solid shape with circles at either end. It has the same circular **cross-section** all along its length.
Tubes, pipes and cans are cylinders.
See also **shape**.

data

Data are numbers and words that you measure or record as part of a project, survey or experiment.

The information and facts stored by a **computer** are called data. Lists of names and addresses are examples of computer data.

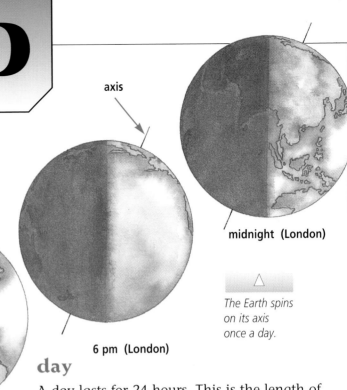

axis

midnight (London)

The Earth spins on its axis once a day.

6 pm (London)

12 noon (London)

6 am (London)

date

A date is a group of numbers or words and numbers which tell you when an event happened or is planned. Some dates are very exact. The spacecraft Apollo 11 landed on the Moon on 23 July 1969. Other dates are more approximate. In 1492 Columbus sailed from Portugal to America.
See also **calendar.**

day

A day lasts for 24 hours. This is the length of time that the Earth takes to make one complete turn on its **axis**. Midnight is the time at which one day ends and the next day starts. The Sun rises and sets once during a day.
See also **time**, **week.**

1995: Channel tunnel between England and France completed.

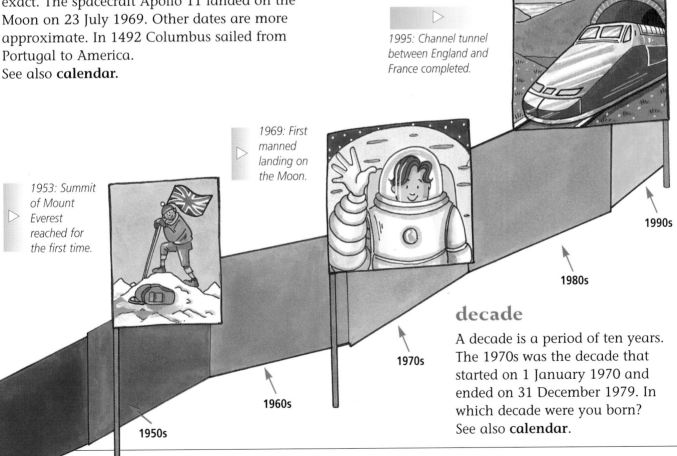

1969: First manned landing on the Moon.

1953: Summit of Mount Everest reached for the first time.

1990s

1980s

1970s

1960s

1950s

decade

A decade is a period of ten years. The 1970s was the decade that started on 1 January 1970 and ended on 31 December 1979. In which decade were you born?
See also **calendar.**

17

decagon

See **shape**.

decimal number

A decimal number is made up of the **digits** from 0 to 9. Decimal numbers are counted in tens. Each digit in the number is ten times higher or lower than the next digit. A decimal point is used to show which digits are whole numbers and which are **fractions**. The digits to the left of the decimal point give the number of units, tens, hundreds and thousands. The digits to the right of the decimal point give the number of tenths, hundredths, thousandths and so on.

degree

A degree is a unit or division on some measuring **scales**. The symbol for degree is °. Degrees are used in temperature scales. The **Celsius** scale is divided into 100 degrees.

Degrees are also used to measure angles. A complete circle is divided into 360 degrees (360°).

The leaning tower of Pisa leans at an angle of 5 degrees.

5 3 6 8.

1000s   100s   10s   1s   decimal point

The digits to the left of the decimal point show the units, tens, hundreds and thousands.

Most countries use decimal coinage. This means that coins are counted in tens or hundreds. In the USA one hundred cents make a dollar. In the UK one hundred pennies make a pound.
See also **money**.

denominator

The denominator is the number below the line in a fraction. In the fraction $\frac{3}{4}$, the denominator is 4.
See also **fraction**.

decimal point

See **decimal number**.

The denominator is the number of parts the whole has been divided into.

diagonal

A diagonal line joins together two corners inside a shape such as a square. The corners joined by a diagonal are not joined by an edge of the shape.

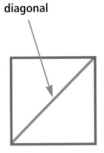

diagonal

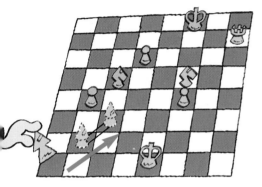

◁ On a chess board the bishops move along diagonal lines of squares.

dice

A dice is a small cube of wood or plastic with the numbers 1 to 6 marked on its faces. The numbers on opposite faces of the dice always add up to 7.

When you roll a dice there is an equal chance of it landing with any one of the numbers on the top face. Dice are used in board games such as snakes and ladders and other games of chance.

See also **probability and statistics**.

◁ The digits to the right of the decimal point show the tenths, hundredths and thousandths.

$\frac{1}{10}$ s $\frac{1}{100}$ s $\frac{1}{1000}$ s

difference

The difference is the number you must count on to get from a smaller number to a bigger one. The difference between 8 and 12 is 4. It is the same as the number you get by taking 8 away from 12. You work out the difference between two numbers by subtracting the smaller one from the bigger one.

See also **subtraction**.

diameter

A diameter is a line that cuts a circle in half. It passes through the centre of the circle. The length of this line is also called the diameter.

The diameter of a **sphere** is the length of the line that passes from one side of the sphere to the other through the centre. Your hat size is the diameter of your head!

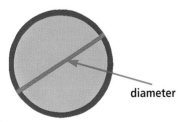

diameter

▷ What is the diameter of your head? The diameter of the inside of your hat must be at least as big, or it will not fit!

digit

A digit is any one of the following: 0, 1, 2, 3, 4, 5, 6, 7, 8 and 9. The number 143 is made up of three digits: 1, 4 and 3.

dimension

The dimensions of an object or shape are its sizes in different directions. For example, the dimensions of a rectangular room might be 5 metres (m) long by 4 m wide by 3 m high.

Shapes and objects can have different numbers of dimensions. A straight line has just one dimension, which we call length. A flat, or plane, shape has two dimensions because it has length and width but no height or thickness. Solid shapes and empty spaces, such as the inside of a room, have three dimensions: length, width and height.
See also **one-dimensional**, **two-dimensional**, **three-dimensional**.

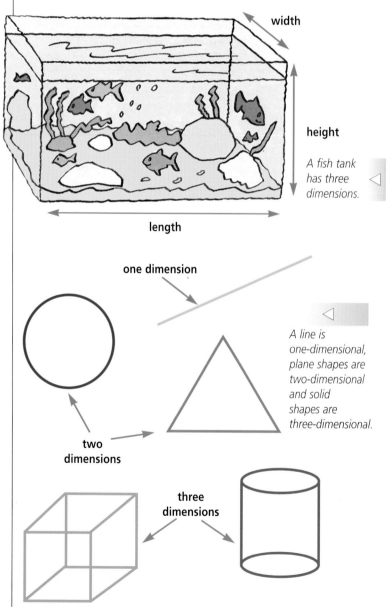

width

height

A fish tank has three dimensions.

length

one dimension

A line is one-dimensional, plane shapes are two-dimensional and solid shapes are three-dimensional.

two dimensions

three dimensions

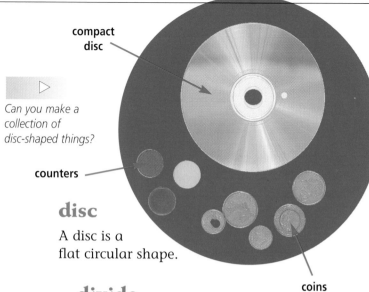

compact disc

Can you make a collection of disc-shaped things?

counters

disc

A disc is a flat circular shape.

coins

divide

Divide means to share out. If you share out 12 pens between three children then you are dividing 12 into three parts. When you divide 12 by 3, the answer is 4. The sign for divide is ÷.

$12 ÷ 3 = 4.$

Each child gets four pens. If you had 14 pens to share, each child would have four pens and there would be two left over:

$14 ÷ 3 = 4$ remainder 2.

See also **division**.

division

Division means finding out how many times one number can be shared out, or divided up, by another number. The answer is called the **quotient**. If the first number cannot be divided exactly by the second number, then there is a remainder.

$14 ÷ 3 = 4$ remainder 2. The quotient is 4.

dodecagon

See **shape**.

dodecahedron

See **shape**.

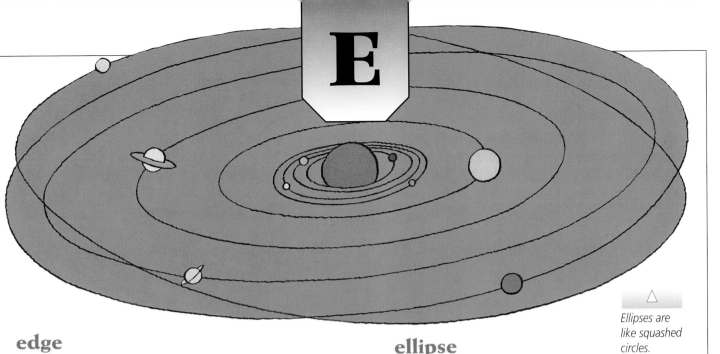

E

edge

An edge is a line that marks the boundary between one thing and another. The edge of a shape shows the outline of that shape.

ellipse

An ellipse is a special oval shape. In space, the planets move around the Sun along invisible paths that are shaped like ellipses. See also **shape**.

△
Ellipses are like squashed circles.

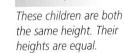

◁ *The two sides of the scale balance. The two weights are equal.*

equal

Equal means 'the same as'. Five plus two equals seven. This means that if you add together the numbers 5 and 2, they are the same as, or equal to, 7. The equals sign is = . It shows that one thing is equal to another: $5 + 2 = 7$.

▽
The edge of the pool is the boundary between solid ground and water.

equal height

▷ *These children are both the same height. Their heights are equal.*

edge

edge

edge

equation

An equation says that one thing is equal to another. Every equation has an equals sign, which shows that the numbers to the left of the sign are the same as, or equal to, the numbers to the right of it.

This simple equation says that two plus three is equal to five:
2 + 3 = 5.

In some equations a letter such as *x* or *y* is used to stand for a number that you do not know.

x = 6 − 2.
What number does *x* stand for in this equation? If *x* = 3, then the equation would not be true. If *x* = 4, then the equation is true.

When you find the value of *x* that makes the equation true, you solve the equation.
See also **algebra, formula.**

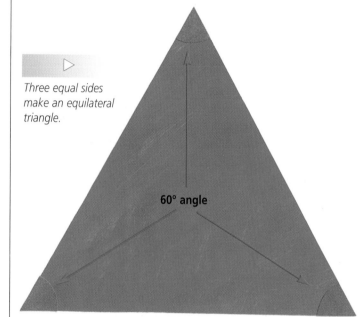

▷
Three equal sides make an equilateral triangle.

60° angle

equilateral triangle

All three sides of an equilateral triangle are the same length. The angles in an equilateral triangle are also all equal. Each one is 60 degrees (60°).
See also **shape.**

estimate

To estimate a number means to decide roughly how much that number is. For example, you might estimate that you need ten bottles of lemonade for a party. If you find that you and your friends drink nine and a half bottles, your estimate was good. If you have six bottles left over after the party, your estimate was poor.
See also **approximate.**

▷
The food and drink estimate for this party was poor!

Euclid

See **famous mathematicians.**

even number

An even number can be divided by 2 without leaving a remainder.

2, 4, 6, 8, 10 . . . are even numbers.
1, 3, 5, 7, 9, 11 . . . are odd numbers.

If you are sharing your felt-tip pens with a friend, it is better to have an even number of pens. Then you can both have the same number of pens and none will be left over.
See also **divide, odd number.**

F

face

A face is one of the flat sides in a solid shape. The faces are surrounded by the shape's edges.

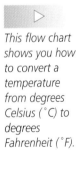

A diamond is cut so that it has many sharp edges and faces.

The buildings in New York have several faces.

factor

A factor is a number that you can **divide** into another number without leaving a remainder. For example, 2 divides into 8 four times with no remainder. So 2 is a factor of 8. What other factors does 8 have?

Ten has three factors (1, 2 and 5), and 12 has five factors (1, 2, 3, 4 and 6). There are three ways to count up to 10 – in ones, twos and fives, but there are five ways to count up to 12 – in ones, twos, threes, fours and sixes.

Fahrenheit

See **temperature**.

famous mathematicians

See pages **24–25**.

flow chart

A flow chart is a diagram that shows the steps you must follow to solve a problem. Flow charts are used to plan computer programs.

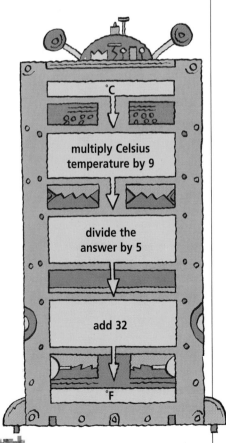

This flow chart shows you how to convert a temperature from degrees Celsius (°C) to degrees Fahrenheit (°F).

°C

multiply Celsius temperature by 9

divide the answer by 5

add 32

°F

Famous mathematicians
(from ancient to modern times)

Pythagoras
(Greece, about 582 – 500 BC)

Pythagoras lived in ancient Greece. He believed that everything in nature including music and beauty could be explained with numbers. Pythagoras' most famous idea was about right-angled triangles.
See also **Pythagoras' theorem**.

Euclid
(Greece, lived about 300 BC)

Euclid made many discoveries about numbers, but he is best known for his books about **geometry**. The geometry of lines and angles that you learn about today was first taught by Euclid more than 2000 years ago.

Euclid proved many things about points, lines, circles and triangles. You learn these when you study geometry.

Archimedes
(Greece, 287 – 212 BC)

Archimedes is best known for his scientific ideas about floating and sinking. According to a story, he ran naked from his bath one day crying 'Eureka!', which means 'I have found it!' He had discovered how to find the **volume** of an object by putting it in water and measuring how much water the object pushed aside. Archimedes was also a great mathematician. He worked out **formulas** for the area of shapes and the volume of solids.

Zu Chong-Zhi and Zu Geng-Zhi
(China, lived about AD 600)

These Chinese mathematicians, who were father and son, calculated the value of **pi** to seven decimal places.

Abu al-Khwarizmi
(Arabia, about AD 780 – 859)

This Arabian mathematician wrote a book that gave the first clear explanation of **algebra**. The book was called *Kitab al-jabr wa muqabalah*, and the word *al-jabr* in its title has given us the modern word 'algebra'.

Leonardo Fibonacci
(Italy, about 1180 – 1250)

Fibonacci was the first mathematician in Europe to use the symbol 0 to mean 'nothing'. He also invented the Fibonacci series of numbers. Each number in the series is equal to the sum of the previous two numbers: 1, 1, 2, 3, 5, 8, 13 . . . Can you continue the series?

John Graunt
(England, 1620 – 1674)

Graunt was the first person to study facts that we would now call **statistics**.
By looking at the written records of deaths in London he discovered that on average women live longer than men. He also found out that about the same number of people die every year.

Archimedes proved that the King's crown was not pure gold. He measured its volume and weighed it. The crown weighed less than the same volume of pure gold.

Blaise Pascal
(France, 1623 – 1662)

Pascal, together with another Frenchman called Pierre de Fermat, invented a set of ideas about **probability**. He also discovered a triangle of numbers which is important in **algebra**. This triangle had been invented centuries earlier by Arabian and Chinese mathematicians.

Each number in Pascal's triangle is found by adding the two numbers above it. Can you find the next row of the triangle?

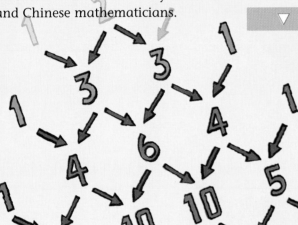

Carl Friedrich Gauss
(Germany, 1777 – 1855)

At the age of 17 Gauss proved that it was impossible to make a regular heptagon (a seven-sided **polygon**) with just a ruler and a compass. But he did find ways to make polygons with 17 257 and 65 537 sides. Gauss became a great scientist and mathematician. He developed many new ideas about numbers, **algebra**, **geometry** and **probability**.

Gauss

Charles Babbage
(England, 1792 – 1871)

Babbage invented the first calculating machine. It was called the 'analytical engine' and was like a mechanical **computer**.

Augusta Ada Byron (Lady Lovelace)
(England, 1815 – 1852)

Lady Lovelace worked with Charles Babbage on his analytical engine. A computer language called 'Ada' is named after her.

Gottfried Wilhelm Leibniz
(Germany, 1646 – 1716)

Leibniz invented an advanced kind of mathematics called 'calculus'. He also built a calculating machine to multiply, divide and find square roots. However, it was not very reliable.

Leonhard Euler
(Switzerland, 1707 – 1783)

Euler studied numbers (including **magic squares**), algebra, equations and **trigonometry**. Although he was almost blind after the age of 20, he still wrote hundreds of books on mathematics during his lifetime.

Pierre Simon, Marquis de Laplace
(France, 1749 – 1827)

Laplace worked out **equations** about the movement of the planets, using Isaac Newton's ideas on **gravity**. He also worked out ideas about **probability**.

George Boole
(Ireland, 1815 – 1864)

George Boole worked out a system called Boolean algebra. It is now used by people who design and program **computers**.

Srinivasa Ramanujan
(India, 1887 – 1920)

Ramanujan taught himself mathematics from textbooks. He had many originals ideas about numbers and thought that every number was interesting.

Euler

foot (ft)

A foot is a measure of length. It has been used since ancient times because the length of a person's foot was an easy way to measure a length of wood or a piece of land.

The size of people's feet varies, so it must have been good to have big feet when buying something! Today a foot is a standard length in the **imperial system** of measurement. See also **measure**.

formula

A formula is a rule that tells you how to work out one thing by combining others. The formula for finding the area of a rectangle is: area = length x width.

fraction

A fraction is a number that is less than a whole number. Half is a fraction. Half a cake is just a part, or a fraction, of the whole cake.

If you cut a pizza into four equal slices then it is divided into quarters. When you take one slice away you are left with three quarters ($\frac{3}{4}$).

Fractions can be written in different ways. A vulgar fraction, such as $\frac{3}{4}$ (three-quarters), is written with a **numerator** and a **denominator**. The denominator is 4. It tells you that the whole has been divided into four equal parts. The numerator is 3. It tells you that there are three parts in the fraction.

A decimal fraction gives the number of tenths, hundredths, thousandths and so on in the fraction. The vulgar fraction $\frac{1}{2}$ is the same as the decimal fraction 0.5.

The digits after the decimal point give the number of tenths, hundredths, thousandths and so on.

$$0.531$$

$\frac{1}{10s}$ $\frac{1}{100s}$ $\frac{1}{1000s}$

A proper fraction is always less than 1. A fraction such as $\frac{3}{2}$ (which is the same as one and a half, or $1\frac{1}{2}$) is called an improper fraction because it is greater than 1.
See also **decimal number**.

frequency table

A frequency table is a way of recording information. It shows the number of different events in a certain amount of time. This is called the 'frequency'.

function

A function is a rule for changing one **set** of numbers into another set. A function might be to multiply each of the numbers in one set by itself to give the numbers in a second set.

This 'function machine' multiplies numbers by themselves. It changes 1 into 1, 2 into 4, 3 into 9 and so on. What does the function do to 4 and 5?

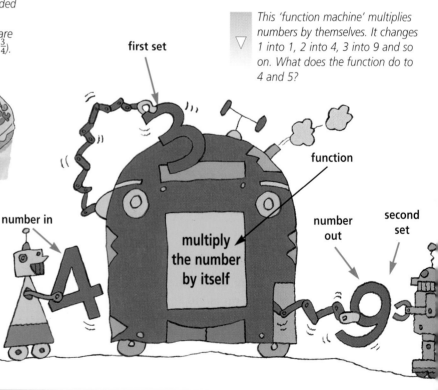

first set

function

number in

multiply the number by itself

number out

second set

G

gallon

A gallon is a measure in the **imperial system**. It measures the amount, or volume, of liquids. A typical plastic bucket holds about two gallons.

geometry

Geometry is the part of mathematics that deals with lines, curves, angles and shapes. Geometrical shapes are made from straight lines, circles and **arcs**.

gram (g)

A gram is a measure of **mass** or weight in the **metric system**. A paper clip has a mass of about one gram (1 g).
See also **measure**.

graph

A graph is a diagram that shows how one thing changes with another. If you plant a seed, you can measure how the height of the seedling changes with time. You can mark the height as a point on a graph. The distance of the point along the **horizontal** axis shows when you measured the seedling. The distance up the **vertical** axis shows the height.

Graph paper is printed with squares to make it easier to mark, or plot, points in the right places. You can plot points with circles or crosses.
See also **bar chart, block graph, scattergram**.

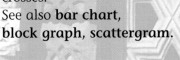

This graph shows how the height of a bean plant changes as the weeks pass.

The design of this door is a pattern made from geometric shapes.
▽

gravity

Gravity is the force that gives objects weight and makes them fall towards the ground.
See also **mass, weight**.

△
The game of battleships is played on a grid. You have to guess in which squares your opponent's ships are hidden.

grid

The grid on a map or plan is a set of numbered or lettered squares. It helps you to find a place by giving the map reference, or **coordinates**, of the place.

height of plant
in centimetres (cm)

50
40
30
20
10

1 2 3 4 5 6
number of weeks

H

I

half

A half is a **fraction**. When something is cut in half it is cut into two equal parts. Two halves of an orange make a whole orange.

hemisphere

A hemisphere is half a **sphere**. It is made by cutting through the centre of a sphere.

hendecagon

See **shape**.

heptagon

See **shape**.

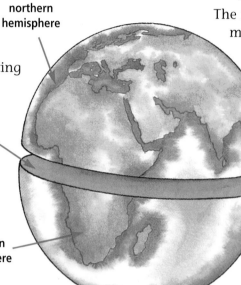

northern hemisphere

equator

southern hemisphere

The equator divides the Earth into the northern and southern hemispheres.

The pattern on this doorway is made up of hexagons.

hexagon

A hexagon is a flat, or plane, shape with six sides.
See also **shape**.

horizontal

When you lie down your body is horizontal. Horizontal means in the same direction as the horizon. The horizon is the faraway line where the land and the sky seem to meet.

hypotenuse

The hypotenuse is the longest side of a **right-angled triangle**.

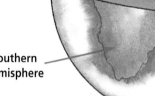

hypotenuse

icosahedron

See **shape**.

imperial system

The imperial, or English, system is a set of measuring units. The system includes measures of length, such as yards, feet and inches; measures of weight, such as pounds and ounces; and measures of **capacity**, such as pints and gallons.

The imperial system was once used throughout the United Kingdom and the United States. In the UK, imperial measures have been officially replaced by metric ones. However, imperial measures are still found in everyday use, for example for distances and speeds on road signs.
See also **measure, metric system**.

inch (in)

An inch is a measure of length in the **imperial system**. One inch is approximately the length of the top section of an adult's thumb.
See also **measure**.

infinity

If you start counting and carry on for ever, there will always be a bigger number than the last one you counted. The number of all the numbers there are is called infinity. The symbol for infinity is ∞.

integer

An integer is another name for a **whole number**. An integer can be a positive number such as 1, 2, 3, etc., or a negative number such as –1, –2, –3, etc. Zero is also an integer.

intersection

An intersection is a crossing point or place. Two lines intersect at a point. Two roads intersect at a junction. The line along which two flat sheets, or planes, cross is also called their intersection.

On a **Venn diagram** the intersection between two **sets** is the area where the sets cross over, or overlap.

isosceles triangle

An isosceles triangle has two equal sides. Two of the angles in an isosceles triangle are always equal.

A junction where two roads meet or cross is called an intersection.
▽

intersection

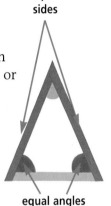

equal
sides

equal angles

An isosceles triangle.

Julian calendar

See **calendar**.

kilogram (kg)

A kilogram is a measure of **mass** in the **metric system**. Kilograms are also commonly used as measures of weight. Ten eating apples weigh about one kilogram (1 kg).
See also **measure**.

kilometre (km)

A kilometre is 1000 metres (m). It is a measure of distance in the **metric system**. It takes about ten minutes to walk one kilometre (1 km).
See also **measure**.

▽ *Road signs in most countries in Europe give distances in kilometres.*

CALAIS 292 Km

L

latitude

Lines of latitude are imaginary circles drawn around the Earth between the Equator and the North and South poles. Together with lines of longitude they make a **grid** on the Earth's surface. We use this grid to find the exact position of a place.

A line of latitude is labelled by the angle it makes with the Equator and the centre of the Earth. The angle is measured in degrees (°). Latitudes above the Equator are labelled 'North', or N; those below the Equator are labelled 'South', or S. See also **longitude**.

length

Length is the distance between the two ends of a line or object.

A length of time is the amount of time from the start of an event to its finish.

light year

A light year is a measure of distance in space. It is the distance that light, the fastest thing in the Universe, travels in one year. One light year is equal to 9.46 trillion kilometres, or 9 460 000 000 000 km. Astronomers use light years to measure the distance to the stars because space is so huge.

The latitude of London in England is 52° north or 52° N. Its longitude is 0°.

London

line of latitude

Rio de Janeiro

line of longitude

Cairo

line

A line is a straight or curved length with no width. A line drawn on paper always has a tiny amount of width, but this is very small if you draw it with a sharp pencil.

litre (l)

A litre is a measure of **capacity** or volume in the **metric system**. Petrol and engine oil are sold in litres.

longitude

Lines of longitude are imaginary circles drawn around the Earth. Each line passes through both the North and South poles. All lines of longitude have the same **radius** as the Earth. Lines of longitude and latitude together make a **grid** on the Earth's surface. We use this grid to find places on a map.

A line of longitude is labelled by the angle it makes with the centre of the Earth and the line that passes through Greenwich in London, England. We call this line the 'Greenwich meridian'. The angle is measured in degrees (°). Longitudes to the right of the Greenwich meridian are labelled 'East', or E; those to the left are labelled 'West', or W. See also **latitude**.

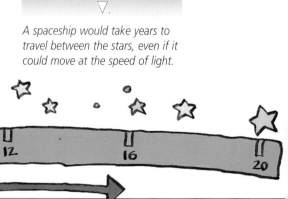

A spaceship would take years to travel between the stars, even if it could move at the speed of light.

4   8   12   16   20
0
light years

M

magic square

A magic square is made up of rows of numbers. If you add together all the numbers in any row, either horizontal, vertical or diagonal, the answer is the same. Some ancient Chinese and Arabic mathematicians believed that these number squares had magic powers.

Check to see if this is a magic square. The three numbers in any line should add up to the same total.
▷

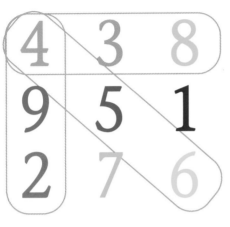

map

A map is a drawing or a diagram of a place such as a town, a country or the whole world. Maps are drawn to **scale**. The distances on a map are much smaller than the real distances. For example, 1 centimetre (cm) on the map of a town could stand for 500 metres (m) in the real town.

To map also means to change one set of numbers into another set by following a rule or **function**.
See also **function, scale.**

▽

A town plan is a map showing the layout of the streets and buildings. Symbols show which buildings are schools, churches or other special places. A grid, a key and a scale help you find places and work out the distance between them.

mass

The mass of an object depends on the amount of material, or matter, in it. An elephant has a larger mass than a mouse. The more massive an object is, then the harder it is to make it move. In the **metric system** mass is measured in kilograms (kg).
See also **weight.**

mathematician

A mathematician is a person who studies mathematics.
See also **famous mathematicians**.

mathematics

Mathematics is the study of numbers, patterns and shapes. We can use mathematics to solve many different kinds of problems.

maximum

The maximum is the largest, the highest or the greatest number in a set of numbers.

mean

The mean of a set of numbers is one way of measuring the average. You find the mean by adding all the numbers together and dividing by how many numbers there are.
See also **average, median, mode.**

Key:

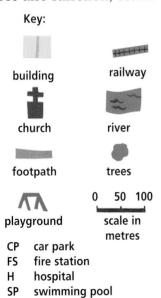

building

railway

church

river

footpath

trees

playground

0   50   100
scale in metres

CP   car park
FS   fire station
H   hospital
SP   swimming pool

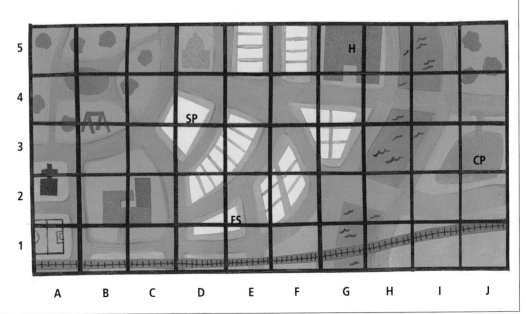

Measure

Measurements are numbers that give us information about the world around us. They help us to buy and sell things, to build roads, to design machines, to cook meals, to get to school on time, to do experiments and to plan what we do each day. Length, weight, temperature and time are different kinds of measure.

Sometimes we need only a rough measure, such as 'a pinch of salt' or 'a few minutes' time'. But other measurements must be very accurate, for example the width of a railway track.

According to the Bible, Noah's ark was 300 cubits long. A cubit is the length from the elbow to the tip of the middle finger of an adult.

▷

Careful measurements have been made of the ancient stone circle of Stonehenge in England. It was probably built using a measure of length that is equal to 0.829 metres. This length is called the megalithic yard.

modern measures

Today, two main systems of weights and measures are used throughout the world. For many years the **imperial system** was used in the USA, the UK and some other countries. Its measures of length were based on the yard (yd). The standard yard was the distance between two lines on a metal bar made in 1845.

The **metric system** of measurement is now the standard system in many parts of the world. The basic measure of length is the metre (m). Mass is measured in kilograms (kg). All other measures of length and mass are found by multiplying or dividing these basic measures by tens, hundreds and thousands. This makes calculations with the metric system much easier than with the imperial system.

the first measures

The first measures were probably rough and ready ones: a hand's width, a pace, a bowlful. Approximate measures like these are still useful when you are doing some jobs.

But builders working together soon realized that they needed a standard measure. With a measure that did not change, they could make everything fit. The foreman probably carried a measuring stick to set the standard.

metric system

measure	unit	symbol
length	metre	m
mass	kilogram	kg
time	second	s

◁

Some basic measuring units and their symbols.

prefixes

prefix	factor	symbol
mega–	1 000 000	M
kilo–	1000	k
hecto–	100	h
deca–	10	da
deci–	1/10	d
centi–	1/100	c
milli–	1/1000	m
micro–	1/1 000 000	μ

◁

A word called a prefix is added to metric measures to make them larger or smaller. This table shows what different prefixes mean.

In the metric system you can make a unit of measure smaller or larger by adding a different word, called a prefix, to the front of a unit. For example, a millimetre (mm) is one-thousandth of a metre, a centimetre (cm) is one-hundredth of a metre, a kilometre (km) is 1000 metres.

measuring instruments

Since the first measuring sticks, scientists and engineers have invented instruments to measure lengths, weights and times more accurately.

Lengths are measured with rulers and tapes. Building surveyors use a tape which gives the measurements on a digital read-out.

Masses and weights are measured with balances and scales.

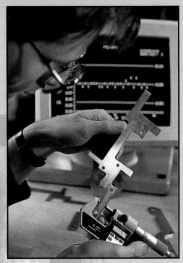

▷

A micrometer measures lengths very accurately. This one has a digital readout.

▷

The foreman on a building site uses modern measuring instruments to check that everything is in the correct place.

▷

A spring balance measures the weight of a newborn baby in kilograms or pounds.

▷

A digital stopwatch measures time. It can show hours, minutes and seconds. Some watches can measure tenths or even hundredths of a second.

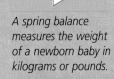

median

The median is the middle, or central, number in a set of numbers. If you line up five children in the order of their heights, the child in the middle has the median height. The median is often close to, but not always the same as, the mean.

median

median

A median is also a line drawn from one corner of a triangle to the middle of the opposite side.
See also **average**, **mode**.

metre (m)

A metre is a measure of length in the metric system. One metre is about the length of a very long stride by an adult.
See also **measure**.

metric system

The metric system is a system of weights and measures. All the units in the metric system are in tens, hundreds and thousands. There are 10 millimetres (mm) in 1 centimetre (cm), 100 cm in 1 metre (m) and 1000 m in 1 kilometre (km). The metric system was invented in France. It is simpler to use than the **imperial system**.
See also **measure**.

micron

A micron is a very small measure of length in the metric system. It is the same as one-millionth of a metre. A human hair is about 100 microns thick. The symbol for micron is μ.
See also **measure**.

mile

A mile is a measure of distance in the imperial system. It takes about 15 minutes to walk one mile.

The distance between the two towers of the Humber Bridge in England is 1.37 miles. It is the longest bridge span in the world.

Scale ruler: 22 23 24 25 26 27 28 29 30 31 32 33 34 35 36 37 38 39 40 41

millennium

A millennium is a period of 1000 years. In the Gregorian calendar, midnight on 31 December 2000 will be the end of the second millennium since the birth of Christ and the start of the third. See also **calendar, time.**

△

This is a centimetre scale. Each centimetre is divided into 10 millimetres.

millimetre (mm)

A millimetre is a small measure of length in the **metric system**. Ten millimetres are equal to one centimetre (cm). See also **measure.**

million

A million is a very large number. It is one thousand thousands, or 1 000 000.

There are three-quarters of a million words in the Bible, about 5 million hairs on a dog and over 30 million seconds in one year.

▷

You can prove that the strip has only one side by drawing a line along the centre. If the strip had two sides you would have to lift your pen to move from one side to the other.

minute

A minute is a length of time. There are 60 seconds in one minute, and 60 minutes in one hour. In one minute you could probably walk the length of a football pitch, whistle 'Happy birthday to you' four times or read a page of this book. See also **time.**

Möbius strip

A Möbius strip is a special shape that you can make from a strip of paper. To make a Möbius strip give one end of the strip half a twist and glue it to the opposite end.

The amazing thing about a Möbius strip is that it only has one side! You can prove this by drawing a line along the centre of the strip without lifting your pen – you will eventually come back to your starting point.

The Möbius strip was discovered by a German mathematician and astronomer called Augustus Ferdinand Möbius (1790 – 1868).

What happens when you cut your Möbius strip in half lengthways? Do you end up with two strips or one?

Try adding extra twists and repeating the experiment.

17

14

19

14

16

14

mode

The mode is the most common number in a set of numbers. It is another measure of **average**, like **median** and **mean**.

The mean number of children in a class is 16. But the most common number of children in a class is 14, so this is the mode.

money

Money is coins, notes or other tokens. It can be swapped for goods or used to pay people to do things. The very first tokens used as money were probably small items such as shells and beads. The oldest known metal coins come from Turkey.

The money in use in a country is called its 'currency'. Different countries have different currencies. In the USA the currency is the dollar, in the UK it is the pound. Banks must agree a value, or rate of exchange, for different currencies. For example, on a certain day 1 pound (£1) may be worth 1.55 US dollars ($1.55).

Coins and notes are tokens. The metal and paper used to make them is worth much less than the value they stand for.

month

A month has between 28 and 31 days. In the Gregorian calendar, which is used by most people in the world, there are 12 months in each year. The length of a month is approximately equal to the time between one New Moon and the next New Moon – 29.5 days.

See also **calendar, time, year**.

multiplication

In a multiplication sum you **multiply** two numbers together. The order of numbers in a multiplication sum does not matter. Six lots of four (4 x 6) is equal to four lots of six (6 x 4).

Multiplication tables help to speed up calculations. If you learn your tables you will quickly know the answers to multiplication sums.

See also **multiplication square**.

Six lots of four (4 x 6) is equal to four lots of six (6 x 4).

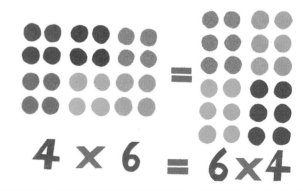

$$4 \times 6 = 6 \times 4$$

multiplication square

A multiplication square contains all the multiplication tables. Every row and column in the square is numbered. If you want to find the answer to 6 x 9, you first find the row for 6. Move along the row of numbers until you reach the square in the column headed 9. The correct answer is in the square where the row for 6 and the column for 9 meet.

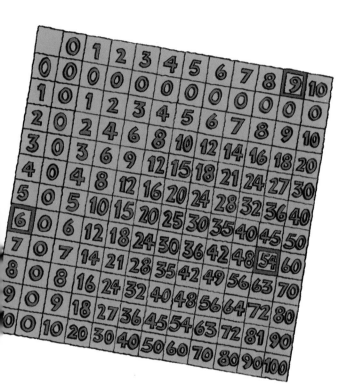

 Does 6 x 9 = 9 x 6? Use the multiplication square to check.

multiply

If you multiply 6 by 4 the answer is 24. To multiply 6 by 4 means to find out what four lots of six equals. The sign for multiply is x:

   6 x 4 = 24.

See also **multiplication.**

negative

A negative number is any number less than zero. The minus sign – is used to show when a number is negative.

How can something be less than nothing? Imagine a quiz game in which you score five points for every correct answer, and lose five points for every wrong one. If you get the first two answers wrong, your score will fall to ten less than zero, or minus ten (–10). You will need two correct answers just to bring your score back to zero.
See also **subtraction.**

net

A net is a flat shape that you can fold to make into a solid shape such as a cube or a pyramid. See also **shape.**

network

A network joins together different places or things. When you draw a network you join things together with lines. Towns and cities are linked by a network of railway lines.

nonagon

See **shape.**

 The telephone network links you to all your friends.

nought

Nought means nothing. It is written as the **digit** 0.

Number

Who first had the idea of counting and making marks to stand for numbers? Early people probably recorded numbers with stone counters, or by making marks on a stick or in a piece of clay. Each counter or mark stood for one thing. Sometimes marks were grouped in fives or sixes to make them easier to count. In time, easier and shorter ways of writing numbers developed.

Roman numerals

The ancient Romans didn't think of using the same number symbol to mean different amounts. Instead, they used different letters for units, tens, hundreds and thousands, and they had no symbol for zero. In Roman numerals 99 is XCIX (See **numeral** for a table of the letters they used.)

Writing Roman numerals takes up much more space than Hindu–Arabic numbers, and doing sums with them is much more difficult. Can you write down the year in Roman numerals?

Counting sheep in prehistoric times. Shepherds must have kept a tally with marks or stones.

This is how the Chinese write the numbers 1 to 10.

The numbers we use today are very clever. With just ten number symbols (0, 1, 2, 3, 4, 5, 6, 7, 8, 9) you can write down huge numbers like 937 615 274 or tiny numbers like 0.000019. The same symbol, or **digit**, means different things depending on its place value, or where it is placed in a number.

This system of numbers was first used in India in the sixth century and was later adopted by Arabian mathematicians. The system of decimal numbers we use today is called the Hindu-Arabic system.

To add numbers with a number line count on to the right. To subtract numbers count back to the left. For example, 7 – 3 = 4.

-6 -5 -4 -3 -2 -1

cardinal and ordinal numbers

When you count the children in your class, or the petals on a flower, you use numbers to find out 'how many' children or petals there are. This kind of number (1, 2, 3) is called a **cardinal number**. But if you count along a row of your friends, the front one is the first, the friend behind is the second, the next friend is the third and so on. This kind of number (1st, 2nd, 3rd) is called an **ordinal number**.

There are six children in the race. Here, 6 is a cardinal number. The boy in the purple shirt is first across the line. Here, 1st is an ordinal number.

3rd   2nd   1st

interesting numbers

The Indian mathematician Srinivasa Ramanujan said that every number is interesting. Here are some interesting facts about the numbers 1 to 9.

1 is the only number that equals itself when you multiply it by itself:

1 x 1 = 1.

2 is the only even **prime number**.

3 is a **triangular number**.

4 is a **square number**: 2 x 2 = 4.

5 is a prime number.

6 is a triangular number. It is also a **perfect number**. It equals the sum of its **factors** (1 + 2 + 3 = 6).

7 is often called 'lucky 7' because it is the most likely, or probable, number when you throw two dice.

8 is a **cubic number**: 2 x 2 x 2 = 8.

9 is a square number: 3 x 3 = 9.

Can you find interesting things to say about the numbers 10 to 20?

number line

A number line shows you the correct order of numbers. It also tells you how big one number is compared to another number. The number 6 is just a bit bigger than 5, but it is twice as big as 3. A number line shows positive and negative numbers.

0 1 2 3 4 5 6 7

numeral

A numeral is a word or a figure that we write down to stand for a number. 'One hundred' is a numeral in words. In Hindu–Arabic numerals the same number is written as 100. In Roman numerals it is C.
See also **number**.

I	1	XXX	30
II	2	XL	40
III	3	L	50
IV	4	LX	60
V	5	LXX	70
VI	6	LXXX	80
VII	7	XC	90
VIII	8	C	100
IX	9	D	500
X	10	CM	900
XX	20	M	1000

This is how the Romans wrote some of the numbers between 1 and 1000. The year 1996 is MCMXCVI.

numerator

The numerator is the number above the line in a fraction. In the fraction $\frac{3}{4}$, the numerator is 3.
See also **fraction**.

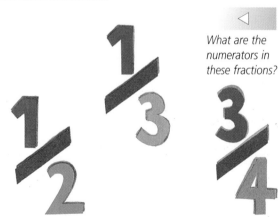

What are the numerators in these fractions?

oblong

Oblong is another word for rectangle.
See also **rectangle**, **shape**.

obtuse angle

An obtuse angle is an angle bigger than a right angle (90 degrees) but smaller than a straight line (180 degrees).

← obtuse angle

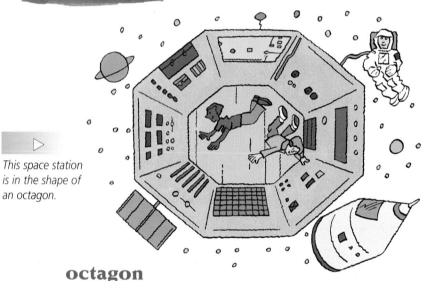

▷
This space station is in the shape of an octagon.

octagon

An octagon is a flat, or plane, shape with eight sides.
See also **shape**.

octahedron

See **shape**.

odd number

Odd numbers are 1, 3, 5, 7, 9, etc. When an odd number is divided by two there is always a remainder of one.

 You cannot divide an odd number of biscuits equally between two children. To avoid an argument, the last biscuit has to be cut in half!

See also **divide**, **even number**.

one-dimensional

A line is one-dimensional because it has length but no width or height. In a one-dimensional world you could only move forwards or backwards. You would not be able to move from side to side, or up and down.
See also **dimension**.

A straight line is one-dimensional.

ordinal number

See **number**.

ounce (oz)

An ounce is a measure of weight in the **imperial system**. In this system there are 16 ounces (oz) in one pound (lb). A small bar of chocolate weighs about 2 oz.
See also **measure**.

oval

An oval is an egg shape or an **ellipse**.

This famous cricket ground in London, England, is called The Oval because of its shape.

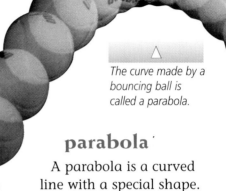

The curve made by a bouncing ball is called a parabola.

parabola

A parabola is a curved line with a special shape.

parallel

Parallel lines are lines that never cross each other. They are the same distance apart along their whole length. Railway lines are parallel.

pattern

A pattern is a special arrangement of numbers or shapes. Patterns repeat or change in a regular way. When you fit simple shapes together in repeating patterns you can make attractive designs.

The pattern of the numbers in some multiplication tables can help you to remember them.

In the five times table, the answer always ends in either 0 or 5. The final **digit** changes between these two numbers. In the nine times table, the final digit is one less each time.

$0 \times 5 = 0$ $0 \times 9 = 0$
$1 \times 5 = 5$ $1 \times 9 = 9$
$2 \times 5 = 10$ $2 \times 9 = 18$
$3 \times 5 = 15$ $3 \times 9 = 27$
$4 \times 5 = 20$ $4 \times 9 = 36$
$5 \times 5 = 25$ $5 \times 9 = 45$

pentagon

A pentagon is a flat, or plane, shape with five sides. See also **shape**.

◁

This building in the United States is called The Pentagon. Can you see why?

percentage

Percentage is another way of giving fractions. You divide something into 100 parts to make a percentage. One per cent of something is one-hundredth part of it. The symbol for percentage is %. One hundred per cent (100%) is the whole; 50% is fifty-hundredths, which is the same as a half; 10% is ten-hundredths, or one-tenth.

To change a vulgar fraction such as $\frac{1}{4}$ or a decimal fraction such as 0.3 into a percentage, you just multiply it by 100:

$\frac{1}{4}$ x 100 = 25%
0.3 x 100 = 30%

perfect number

A perfect number is a number whose **factors** add up to the number itself. The first three perfect numbers are 1, 6 and 28.

The factors of 6 are 1, 2 and 3.
1 + 2 + 3 = 6.

Can you check that 28 is a perfect number?

perimeter

The perimeter is the edge, or boundary, of an area. An airfield or an army camp is often surrounded by a perimeter fence. The perimeter of a curved shape is the same as its **circumference**.

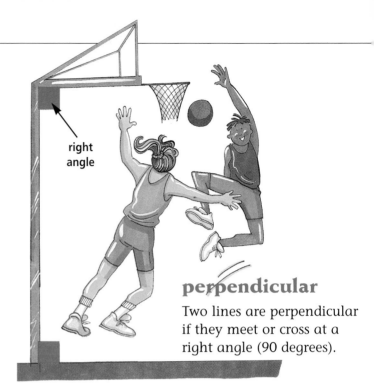

right angle

perpendicular

Two lines are perpendicular if they meet or cross at a right angle (90 degrees).

pi

Pi is a number just bigger than three. If you divide the **circumference** of a circle by its **diameter** then the answer is always pi. The symbol for pi is π. The interesting thing about π is that it cannot be written down exactly. It is approximately 3.1415926, but the **digits** after the decimal point go on for ever. You would need a book with an **infinite** number of pages to write the exact value of π!

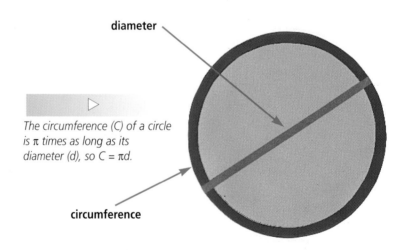

diameter

▷

The circumference (C) of a circle is π times as long as its diameter (d), so C = πd.

circumference

More than 1500 years ago, Chinese mathematicians managed to work out the value of π to seven digits after the decimal point. Today high-speed computers have calculated π to more than 6 billion decimal places.

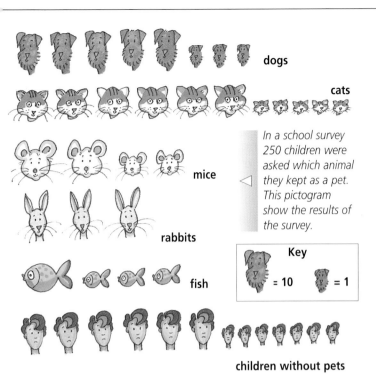

dogs

cats

mice

rabbits

fish

children without pets

In a school survey 250 children were asked which animal they kept as a pet. This pictogram show the results of the survey.

Key

= 10   = 1

pint (pt)

A pint is a measure of **capacity** in the **imperial system**. Eight pints make a gallon. Two soft drinks cans or a medium-sized bottle hold about one pint of liquid. See also **measure**.

pixel

See **computer**.

place value

The place value is the position, or place, of a **digit** in a number. The same digit has a different value at different places in the number. In the number 999, the digit 9 can mean nine hundreds, nine tens or nine units, depending on its place. See also **decimal number**, **number**.

pictogram

A pictogram shows information in pictures or symbols, instead of words and numbers. Each symbol stands for a certain number or amount of something. The meaning of the symbols is shown by a key. Pictograms are used on maps and charts.

This pie chart is another way of showing the results of the pet survey. Here you can see that about a quarter of the children in the survey have a cat.

pie chart

A pie chart shows how something is shared out or divided up. It is drawn as a circle that is divided up into parts, like a pie cut into slices. A pie chart might be used instead of a pictogram to show what pets children have.

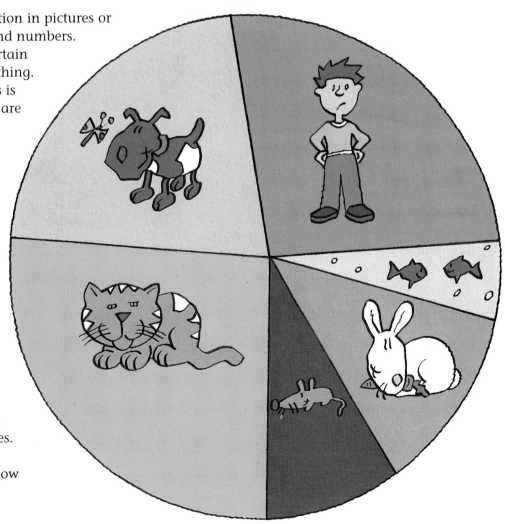

plan

A plan is a drawing or design for an object or building such as an aircraft or a house. Plans usually show views of the object or building from different angles. They often show **cross-sections**. Plans also include measurements and a list of the building materials needed.

A plan view is a drawing of an object or place as seen from above.

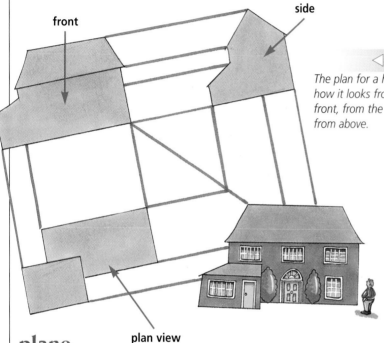

The plan for a house shows how it looks from the front, from the side and from above.

plane

A plane is a flat surface with no ripples, curves or bumps. On a still morning the surface of a lake is an almost perfect plane.

Plane shapes have length and width, but no thickness. We call them **two-dimensional**. Shapes cut from card are almost plane shapes, but they do have some thickness (of the card itself).
See also **shape**.

point

A point is a tiny dot or mark on a graph or a map. It marks a place or a location.

In **geometry** two lines cross at a point. A perfect point is so fine that it has a position but no size at all. It is so tiny that it is impossible to draw.

polygon

A polygon is a flat, or plane, shape with many sides. A hexagon is a polygon with six sides.
See also **shape**.

polyhedron

See **shape**.

The surface of a still lake is like a mirror. It is an almost perfect plane surface.

The positions of these runners are first, second and third.

position

The position of an object is its place or location. On a map, the position of a church is marked with a cross.

Position can also mean the order in which things are placed. The top three positions in a race are first, second and third.

The value of a **digit** in a number depends on its place, or position, in that number. In the number 37 the 3 means three tens (30). But in the number 73 the 3 means three units. See also **place value**.

positive

A positive number is any number above zero. The plus sign + is sometimes used to show when a number is positive, for example +3. See also **negative**.

pound (lb) (£)

A pound is a measure of weight in the **imperial system**. The symbol for pound is lb. Four eating apples weigh about 1 lb.

A pound is also an amount of money in the UK. One hundred pence make one pound. The symbol for a pound in money is £. You can buy about four small packets of crisps with £1. See also **measure, money**.

prime number

A prime number is any whole number, apart from 1, that can *only* be divided by itself and by 1 without leaving a remainder. The first four prime numbers are 2, 3, 5 and 7. Can you write down the next four?

You need a very powerful computer to find out if a large number is a prime number. The largest known prime number has more than 65 000 **digits**.

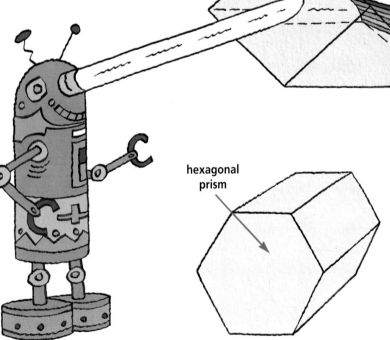

triangular prism

A glass triangular prism can separate white light into the colours of the rainbow.

hexagonal prism

prism

A prism is a solid shape with matching ends. The ends are shaped like triangles, squares or **polygons**. A prism has the same **cross-section** all the way along its length.

Probability and statistics

We know some things for certain. The Sun will rise tomorrow. But other things may or may not come true. It might rain tomorrow, but it might not. In mathematics probability looks at things that are not certain, such as the chance of it raining.

Statistics are facts that we collect to see how the world is changing, for example weather records. Sometimes statistics can help us predict the probability of things happening in the future.

Suppose you stopped the next person you met in the street and asked them some questions. What do you think are the chances that they . . .

. . . are less than 125 years old?
. . . are right-handed?
. . . are female?
. . . are vegetarian?
. . . share your birthday?
. . . come from the planet Mars?

No one lives for more than 125 years and so it is certain (probability 1) that the person will be less than 125 years old. About 9 out of 10 people are right-handed, so the probability that the next person you meet is right-handed is $\frac{9}{10}$ or 0.9. The probability that they are female is about $\frac{1}{2}$ or 0.5, because there are approximately equal numbers of men and women. There is no life on Mars – probability 0!

◁ *An old saying says that lightning never strikes twice in the same place, but statistics prove that sometimes it does.*

probability

Probability is the mathematical word for chance. We can write down the probability that something will happen as a **fraction**. If something is certain to happen its probability is 1. If something is certain not to happen, its probability is 0. If there is an even (one in two) chance that something will happen, like a coin landing on 'heads' when you toss it, then the probability is $\frac{1}{2}$ or 0.5.

▷ *There is a good chance that the next person you meet is right-handed. The probability that they share your birthday is much smaller.*

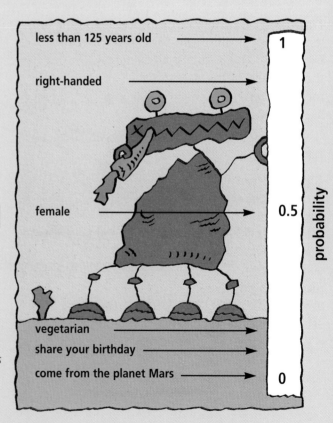

less than 125 years old → 1

right-handed →

female → 0.5

vegetarian →
share your birthday →
come from the planet Mars → 0

probability

a fair chance

The probability of throwing a six with a dice is one chance in six (1 in 6). This is because there are six faces on the dice, and each face has an equal chance of being on top after one throw. After a few throws some numbers may have come up much more often than others, just by chance. But after many throws each number will have come up roughly the same number of times.

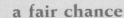

statistics

Statistics are groups of numbers and words that give information about people and things. This information could be the test results for the children in different schools, the numbers of people watching certain television programmes, the most popular makes of car, or the average rainfall in different parts of the country.

Statistics can be very valuable. For example, we know that smoking is dangerous because statistics show that smokers have more illnesses than non-smokers.

collecting statistics

Statistics are collected in surveys. In a consumer survey shoppers are asked which products they buy, and why they prefer some products to others. The store owners use the statistics to decide what products to sell to try to increase their chances of attracting customers into the store.

Governments collect statistics about all the people in a country in a giant survey called a census. Every adult has to fill in a form, giving information about their home, family, age, occupation and income. These statistics help the government plan for the future.

▷

Statistics record the heights, weights and ages of children in a school. You could collect statistics like these to find the average height and weight of children in your class.

name	sex	height (metres)	weight (kg)
Simon	m	1.30	29
Jane	f	1.27	26
Josie	f	1.31	31
Paul	m	1.33	34
Steven	m	1.35	30
Paula	f	1.32	30

▷

Television viewing statistics show which programmes are most popular. The television companies collect them every week.

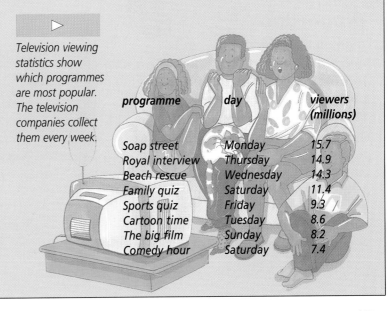

programme	day	viewers (millions)
Soap street	Monday	15.7
Royal interview	Thursday	14.9
Beach rescue	Wednesday	14.3
Family quiz	Saturday	11.4
Sports quiz	Friday	9.3
Cartoon time	Tuesday	8.6
The big film	Sunday	8.2
Comedy hour	Saturday	7.4

product

The product is the answer you get when you multiply together two or more numbers. The product of 2 and 3 is 6 (2 x 3 = 6). See also **multiply**.

projection

A projection of a solid shape is a drawing on a flat sheet. The drawing is made by imagining parallel lines coming from different points in the object. These lines stick out, or project, to meet the sheet of paper at right angles.

Another way to make a projection is to imagine lines coming from a point, passing through the object and then cutting the paper. This gives a different view of the object.

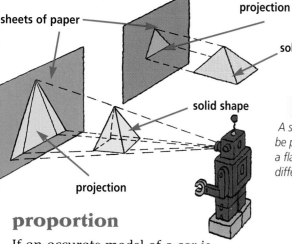

sheets of paper

projection

solid shape

solid shape

projection

A solid shape can be projected on to a flat sheet in different ways.

proportion

If an accurate model of a car is one-fifth of the length of the real car, the model steering-wheel must be one-fifth the size of the real steering-wheel. We say that the model car is in proportion to the real car.

The numbers 5 and 15 are in the same proportion as the numbers 1 and 3 because 5 is one-third of 15, and 1 is one-third of 3. See also **ratio**, **scale**.

protractor

A protractor is an instrument for measuring and marking out angles. It has a **scale** that is marked in degrees.

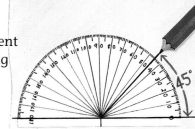

pyramid

A pyramid is a solid shape with triangular faces. The faces meet at a point called the **vertex**. The base of the pyramid can be shaped like a triangle, a square or any **polygon**.

The great pyramid of Giza was built about 2570BC – about 4600 years ago.

Pythagoras

See **famous mathematicians**.

Pythagoras' theorem

Pythagoras' theorem is one of the most famous discoveries in geometry. It is a rule about **right-angled triangles**. First, square (multiply by itself) the lengths of the two shorter sides of a right-angled triangle. Then add them together. Your answer will be the same as when you square the length of the longest side, the **hypotenuse (h)**.

a

h

b

Count the squares on the sides of this right-angled triangle. You should find that $5^2 = 4^2 + 3^2$. ($h^2 = a^2 + b^2$).

Q

quadrant

A quadrant is one-quarter of a circle.

A quadrant is also the name given to each of the four areas on a graph. The graph is divided into four quadrants by its axes.

A surveyor's quadrant is a kind of **protractor**. It is used to measure angles up to 90 degrees (°). See also **axis**.

radius

quadrant

quadrilateral

A quadrilateral is a flat, or plane, shape with four sides.
See also **shape**.

quadruple

Quadruple means to multipy by four. If your pocket money is quadrupled, then you will get four times as much money.

quarter

When something is divided into quarters it is divided into four equal parts.
One-quarter ($\frac{1}{4}$) is one-fourth part of a whole.
See also **fraction**.

quotient

The quotient is the number of times that one number will **divide** into another number. It is the whole number part of the answer to a **division** sum. In the sum $9 \div 2 = 4.5$, the quotient is 4.

R

radius

The radius is the length of a straight line from the centre of a circle to its **circumference**.

random

Random means purely by chance. Random numbers, for example those drawn in a lottery or thrown with dice, have an equal chance of coming up each time a selection is made.

In a lottery numbered balls are drawn at random from a drum. The probability that the numbers match those on your ticket is very very small.

ratio

If a scale model boat is one-tenth of the size of a real boat, the model boat is one-tenth as long as the real boat. We say that their lengths are in the ratio one to ten. We write this as $1 : 10$.

The scale of a map is a ratio. On a map with a scale of $1 : 100\ 000$, 1 centimetre (cm) on the map stands for a real distance of 100 000 cm, which is 1 kilometre (km).
See also **fraction**, **proportion**.

rectangle

A rectangle is a four-sided flat, or plane, shape. Its sides join at right angles.
See also **area**.

recurring

Recur means repeat. If you use your calculator to do the calculation 1 ÷ 3 you get the answer 0.3333333333. The line of threes would fill your calculator display panel no matter how long it was. This answer is called 'nought point three recurring' and it is sometimes written as 0.ȯ3. The dot over the ȯ3 shows that it recurs. Can you use your calculator to find other recurring decimals?

reflection

Your reflection in the mirror looks almost exactly the same as you, but not quite. When you raise your right hand your reflection raises its left hand. Reflection swaps right and left.

A shape with two sides that are mirror images has reflection **symmetry**. If you place a mirror along the centre of a butterfly, the reflection of the right side looks exactly like the left side.

Some letters like O have reflection symmetry. They look exactly the same in a mirror. Other letters like K look back to front in a mirror.

reflex angle

A reflex angle is an angle bigger than 180 degrees (180°)

remainder

See **divide, division**.

rhombus

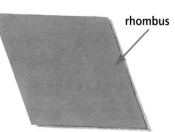

rhombus

A rhombus is a flat, or plane, diamond shape. It is a **quadrilateral** with four equal sides.

right angle

An angle of 90 degrees (90°) is called a right angle. If you turn all the way around then you have turned through four right angles.
See also **perpendicular**.

right angle

The corner of a football pitch is a right angle. A groundsman can use a rope with equally spaced knots to draw it out.

▷

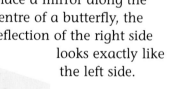

right-angled triangle

A right-angled triangle has one angle of 90 degrees (90°). A triangle with sides that measure 3, 4 and 5 centimetres (cm) is a right-angled triangle. If the sides of a triangle are in the **ratio** of 3 : 4 : 5, the triangle is always a right-angled one.

Roman numeral

See **number, numeral**.

A square looks the same after one quarter of a turn.

An equilateral triangle looks the same after one third of a turn.

rotation

A rotation means a turn. A complete turn always brings a shape back to its startin-point. The shape rotates by 360 degrees (360˚). We say that shapes like squares and equilateral triangles have rotational **symmetry** because they look the same after less than a full turn.

rounding

Rounding a decimal fraction means writing it with fewer **digits**. When you use a calculator, the answer often has more digits than you need. The last digit you want to keep is rounded up if the digits you don't want start with a 5 or more. The last digit stays the same if the digits you don't want start with a number less than 5.

You can round the number 4.761 to 4.8. The 7 changes to 8 because the digits you don't want start with a number more than 5. How would you round the number 4.736?

row

A row is a line of objects, one after the other. In a table of numbers the rows are the horizontal lines of numbers. The vertical lines of numbers are called 'columns'.

column

1	2	3	4	5
6	7	8	9	10
11	12	13	14	15

row ⟶

ruler

A ruler is a straight-edged stick with a **scale** marked along it. You use a ruler to measure lengths and to draw straight lines.

ruler

scale

A scale is a series of steps or degrees that we use to measure something. The scale on a ruler is marked in centimetres (cm) and millimetres (mm). The scale on a thermometer shows the temperature in degrees (°).

The scale of a model or a **plan** gives its size compared to the real thing. A 1:10 scale drawing of a house is one-tenth of the size of the real house. So a window pane that measures 100 cm in the real house measures 10 cm on the drawing. See also **conversion, ratio**.

▷ *The scale on this machine shows your weight.*

scattergram

A scattergram is a kind of **graph**. When you draw, or plot, the points on a scattergram they will be scattered across the graph. On a graph of shoe sizes for children of different ages, the points are scattered about because children of the same age wear different-sized shoes.

▷ *This scattergram gives the shoe sizes of 40 children, aged 5 to 11 years. It shows that children's feet grow by one to two sizes a year.*

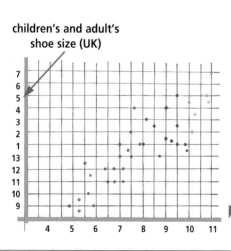

children's and adult's shoe size (UK)

age (years)

second

A second is an amount of time. It takes about one second to say the word 'second'. There are 60 seconds in one minute.

The second thing in a list is the next thing after the first.

section

A section is a slice through an object. You can make a section through an object at different angles. A section through a cone is either a circle, an **ellipse** or a **parabola**. See also **cross-section**.

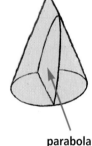

▷ *You can slice through a cone at different angles to make different shaped sections.*

ellipse

parabola

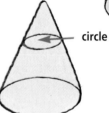

circle

sector

A sector of a circle is like a slice taken from the circle by making two cuts.

▷ *The curved edge of a sector is an arc. Each of the two straight edges is a radius.*

sector

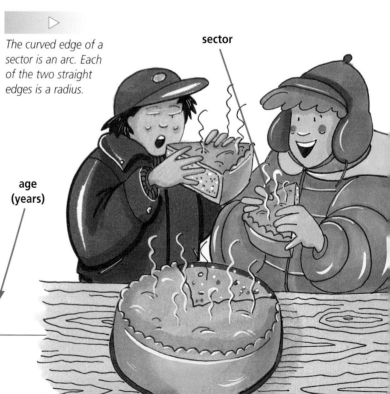

The curved edge of a segment is an arc. The straight edge is a chord.

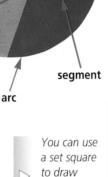

chord

segment

arc

segment

A segment of a circle is like a piece taken off the circle with a single cut. An orange segment is a segment of a **sphere** – the orange.

semicircle

A semicircle is half a circle.

sequence

A sequence is a row or line of numbers. The next number in a sequence is found by applying a rule to the previous number. For example, in the sequence 1 4 7 10 13 16 the next number is found by adding 3 to the previous number.

Can you find the rules to continue these sequences?
1 2 4 8 16 32 . . .
2 4 16 256 . . .
1 1 2 3 5 8 13 21 . . .

set square

A set square is a triangular piece of metal or plastic used for drawing. One angle of the set square is a right angle, so you can draw **perpendicular** lines with it. The other angles are usually both 45 degrees (45°), or sometimes one is 30° and the other 60°.

You can use a set square to draw right angles on drawings and plans.

set

A set is a group of numbers, shapes or objects with a particular thing in common. The numbers 1, 2, 3, 4, 5, 6, 7, 8 and 9 are the set of whole numbers less than 10. This set can be written as (1, 2, 3, 4, 5, 6, 7, 8, 9). It can be split into two smaller sets: even numbers and odd numbers. See also **Carroll diagram**, **Venn diagram**.

Some names are girls' names. Some names are boys' names. Some names are both boys' and girls' names. Names can be sorted into two sets that overlap.

boys' names

George

Raul   Joshua

Sunil

Sam   Pip

Alex

boys' and girls' names

Rose   Yasmin

Sumila   Julie

girls' names

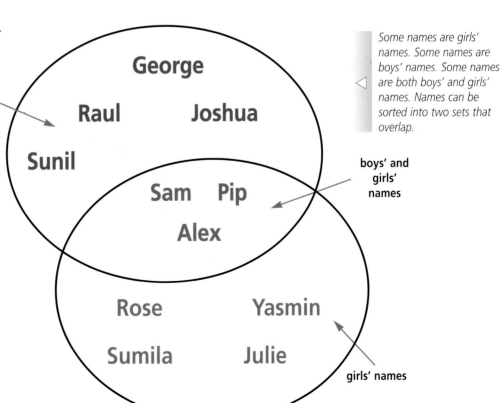

Shape

Every object has a shape. A rock has an irregular shape and so does a potato crisp. But objects like bricks and balls are regular shapes with mathematical names. In mathematics, shapes are drawn with lines to show their edges or sides. Many shapes have names which describe how many edges they have or whether the edges are curved or straight.

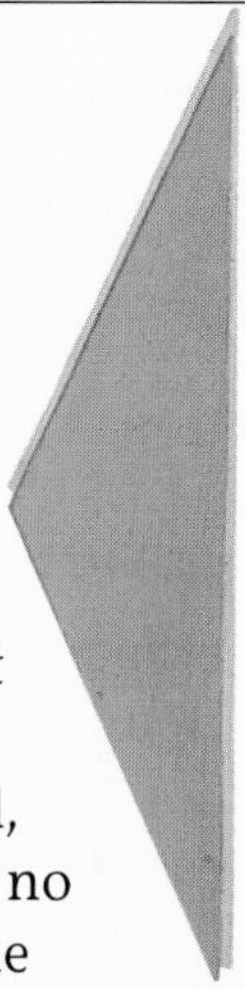

triangles

plane shape

A plane shape is a flat shape that can be cut from a sheet of paper. It can have straight or curved edges. Plane shapes are **two-dimensional**, so they have length and width but no height or thickness. A triangle is the simplest plane shape with straight edges. It has just three sides. A quadrilateral is a plane shape with four sides.

These plane shapes have straight edges.

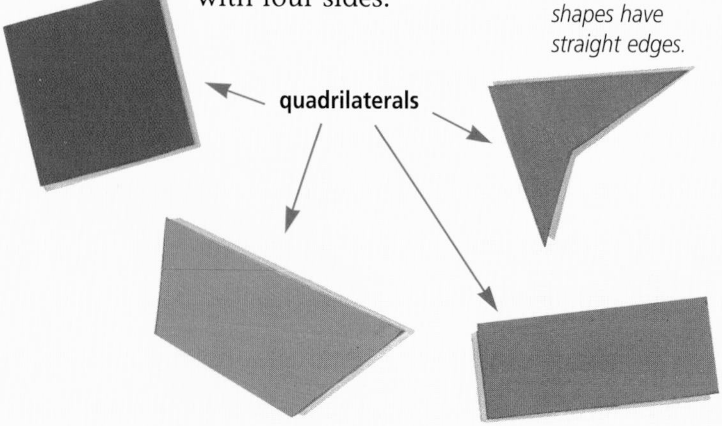

polygon

A polygon is any shape with three or more straight sides. When all the sides and angles of a polygon are equal, we call that shape a regular polygon.

Number of sides	Name of polygon
3	triangle
4	quadrilateral
5	pentagon
6	hexagon
7	heptagon
8	octagon
9	nonagon
10	decagon
11	hendecagon
12	dodecagon

quadrilaterals

circle

These plane shapes have curved edges.

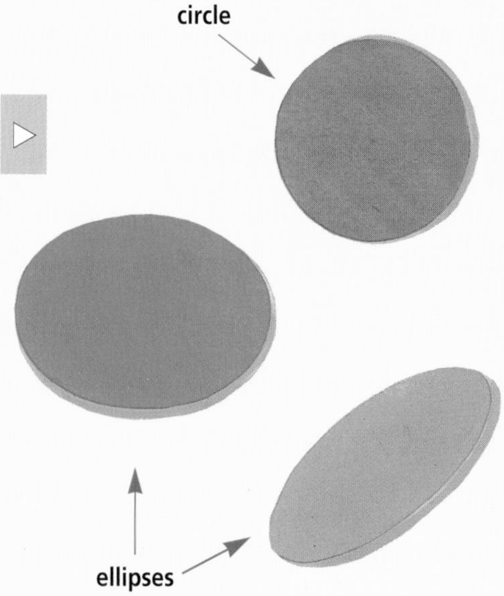

These plane shapes are polygons. Each one has a different number of edges.

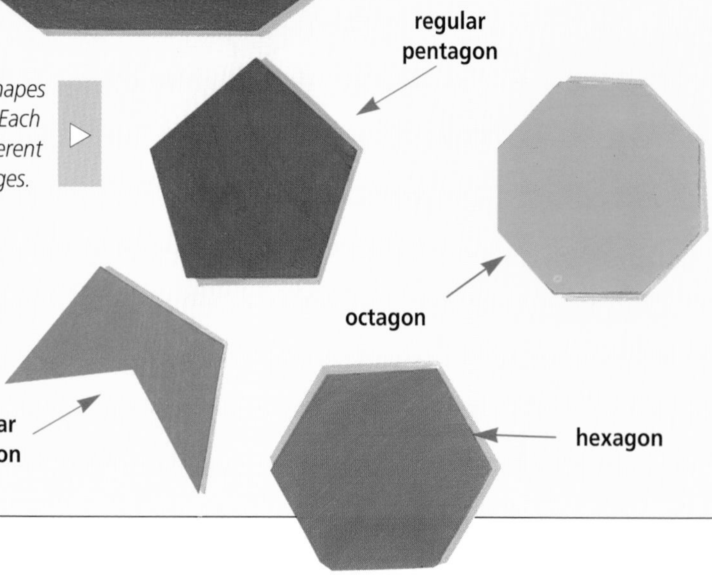

regular pentagon

octagon

ellipses

irregular pentagon

hexagon

solid shape

A solid shape is **three-dimensional**. It has length, width and height (thickness). The flat part of a solid shape is called a face.

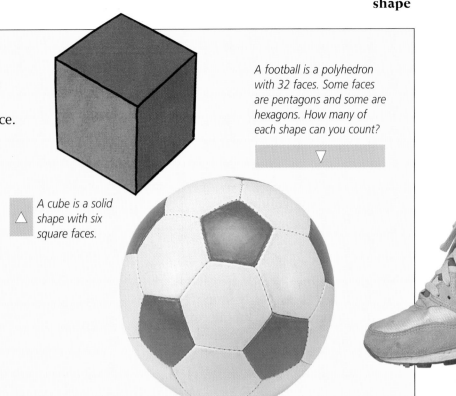

A cylinder has circular ends and the same circular cross-section all along its length. ◁

A cube is a solid shape with six square faces. △

A football is a polyhedron with 32 faces. Some faces are pentagons and some are hexagons. How many of each shape can you count? ▽

Some solid shapes with curved edges have special mathematical names. ▽

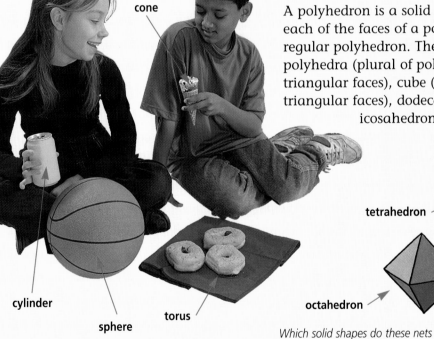

cone

cylinder

sphere

torus

polyhedron

A polyhedron is a solid shape with straight edges. When each of the faces of a polyhedron is identical, we call it a regular polyhedron. There are only five different regular polyhedra (plural of polyhedron): **tetrahedron** (4 triangular faces), cube (6 square faces), octahedron (8 triangular faces), dodecahedron (12 pentagonal faces) and icosahedron (20 triangular faces).

cube

tetrahedron

dodecahedron

octahedron

icosahedron

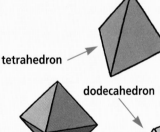

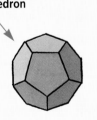

net

A net shows you what a solid shape would look like if you could lay it out flat. You can draw a net on a piece of card or paper. Cut out the shape, then fold and glue it to make a regular solid shape, such as a cube or a pyramid.

Which solid shapes do these nets make? (The dotted lines show you where to fold the paper.) Can you make a net for an octahedron? ▽ ▷

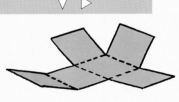

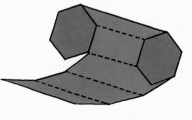

space

All objects take up space. Space is emptiness waiting to be filled. Two objects cannot fill the same space. The amount of space things fill depends on their size or volume. The amount of space inside an empty box depends on the three dimensions of the box: its length, width and height.
See also **capacity**, **volume**.

speed

Speed tells you how fast something is moving. Speed is how far you move in a certain amount of time. People can walk at a speed of about six kilometres (km) an hour. At this speed it takes one hour to walk 6 km, or 10 minutes to walk 1 km.

This 'space' entry fills the space inside the box.

square

A square is a flat, or plane, shape with four straight and equal sides. The angles in its corners are all **right angles**.

A square has four equal sides and four equal angles.

The square of a number is the number when multiplied by itself. The square of two, or two squared, is 2 x 2 = 4. You can show that a number is squared by writing a small number 2 just after and above the number: 2^2.
See also **square number.**

square number

A square number can be arranged as a group of dots in the shape of a square. The number of dots is the same as the number itself. The first four square numbers are 1, 4, 9 and 16. Can you work out the next four?

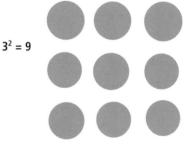

$1^2 = 1$

$2^2 = 4$

$3^2 = 9$

$4^2 = 16$

The Earth is almost a perfect sphere but not quite. It is slightly flattened at the poles and it bulges slightly at the Equator. This shape is called a spheroid.

sphere

A sphere is a solid shape with a curved surface. It is a perfect shape because every place on the surface of a sphere is exactly the same distance from its centre.

spheroid

A spheroid is a slightly squashed sphere.
See also **sphere**.

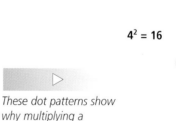

These dot patterns show why multiplying a number by itself is called 'squaring'.

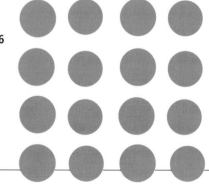

square root

The square root of a number is the number that, when multiplied by itself, gives you the first number. Two is the square root of four. So when two is squared (2 x 2), the result is four. The symbol for square root is √. √ 4 = 2.

statistics

See **probability and statistics**.

straight line

A straight line is the shortest distance between two points. It has no curves or bends. A curved line between two points is always longer than a straight one.

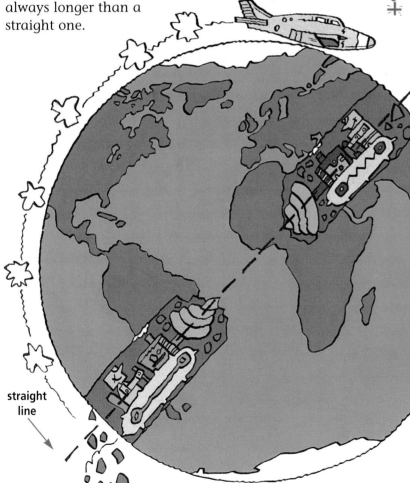

straight line

subtraction

Subtraction means taking one number away from another. If the number 5 is taken away from the number 9, the answer is 4. The minus sign – is used to show when one number is subtracted from another. For example, 9 – 5 = 4.

If a large number is subtracted from a smaller one, the answer is a **negative** number.

10 – 20 = -10.
If the temperature during the day is 10 °C, and the temperature then drops by 20 °C at night, the temperature during the night is -10 °C.

sum

The sum of two or more numbers is the answer you get when you add them together.

The sum of 2 and 3 is 5:
2 + 3 = 5.

Sums are the **arithmetic** work you do at school when you add, subtract, divide or multiply numbers.
See also **addition**.

surface

The surface of an object is its outside layer or boundary. When you paint a door, you spread the paint on to the door's surface. The surface of your body is covered by your skin.
See also **area**.

A journey between two places on the Earth's surface is always curved. It would be shorter to travel along a straight line, but that would mean digging a tunnel through the Earth!

The surface of a pond is the boundary between the water and the air. Some insects are light enough to stand on a water surface.

Symmetry

A shape has symmetry when two or more of its parts are matching shapes.

There are different kinds of symmetry. If an object looks exactly the same when it is turned by an angle less than 360 degrees (360°) it has 'rotational symmetry'.

If one half of a shape is the 'mirror image' of the other half then the shape has 'mirror symmetry' or 'reflection symmetry'. If you place a mirror along the line separating the two halves the shape looks unchanged.

This butterfly has mirror symmetry but it does not have rotational symmetry.

This symmetrical cross looks the same if you turn it by 90°. It has rotational symmetry.

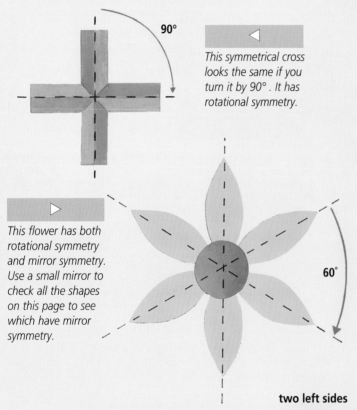

This flower has both rotational symmetry and mirror symmetry. Use a small mirror to check all the shapes on this page to see which have mirror symmetry.

If a pattern is repeated so that it looks the same when it is moved along by a set amount, then it has 'translation symmetry'. The patterns on carpets and wallpaper often have translation symmetry.

Some letters of the alphabet are symmetrical. The letter **W** has mirror symmetry. The letter **Z** has rotational symmetry. Which are the other symmetrical letters?
See also **reflection, rotation, translation.**

How different are the left and right sides of your face? Would you look better with two 'right' faces or two 'left' faces?

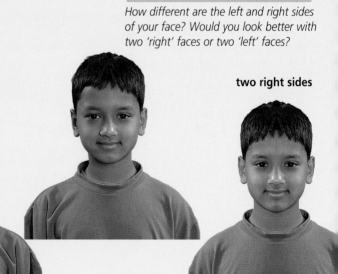

two left sides

two right sides

Most human faces are almost symmetrical, but not quite. Try placing a mirror on a photograph of your face to see what you would look like with two 'left' or two 'right' halves to your face.

T

table

A table is a list of numbers in rows and columns. It can show information that has been collected in a survey, the results of a science experiment or the scores in a game.

	Played	Won	Drawn	Lost	Points
Rovers	10	8	1	1	25
City	9	8	0	1	24
Rangers	11	6	3	2	21
United	10	5	2	3	17
Albion	9	5	1	3	16

△ A football league table shows the games won, drawn and lost by the different teams. In this league the teams score 3 points for a win, 1 point for a draw and 0 points for a loss.

take away

See **subtraction**.

tally

A tally is a count of numbers. You can keep a tally with marks when you are counting cars in a traffic survey or the number of runs in a game of cricket.

tangent

A tangent is a straight line that just touches a curve but does not cross over it.

A spinning wheel throws off mud and water at a tangent to its circumference. ▽

tangent

temperature

Temperature tells you how hot or cold something is. When you switch on an oven its temperature rises. Temperature is measured in degrees (°) as a number on a scale. The most common temperature scales are the **Celsius** (˚C) scale and the **Fahrenheit** (˚F) scale.

▽ On the Celsius temperature scale ice melts at 0 ˚C and water boils at 100 ˚C. On the Fahrenheit scale ice melts at 32 ˚F and water boils at 212 ˚F.

surface of the sun 5527 ˚C

wood burns 250 ˚C

water boils 100 ˚C

water freezes 0 ˚C

air liquifies −200 ˚C

LIQUID AIR

tessellation

A tessellation is a repeating pattern of plane shapes. It is made by fitting the shapes together to cover a surface completely. The patterns made by paving stones are tessellations.

You can make tessellations with triangles, squares, rectangles and hexagons. Some shapes will not fit together to cover a whole surface. When you fit together regular pentagons, there are always gaps that show the surface below.

The word 'tessellation' comes from the Latin word *tessera*. A *tessera* was one of the small blocks of coloured stone which the Romans used to make mosaics.

△ This drawing by the artist Escher (1902–1973) is a tessellation of irregular shapes.

tetrahedron

A tetrahedron is a solid shape with four triangular faces.

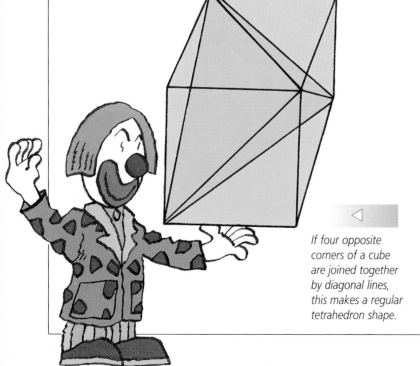

◁ If four opposite corners of a cube are joined together by diagonal lines, this makes a regular tetrahedron shape.

third

A third is one of the parts you make when you divide something into three equal parts.

In a row of trees, the third tree is the next one after the first and second trees. See also **fraction**.

△ Volleyball is a game in three dimensions. The ball can move up and down, left and right and forwards and backwards as it crosses the net.

three-dimensional

A solid shape is three-dimensional (3-D) because it has length, width and height. Our world is three-dimensional because you can move anywhere by combining moves along just three lines: backwards and forwards, left and right, up and down. See also **dimension**, **space**.

When it is midday in London, England, it is 7 am in New York, USA and 9 pm in Tokyo, Japan.

time

A clock measures time in hours, minutes and seconds. The hour hand makes one complete turn of the clock every twelve hours. Midday, or 12 noon, divides each day into two parts. Any time before midday is known as am (*ante meridian*). Seven o'clock in the morning is 7 am. Times after noon are pm (*post meridian*). Six o'clock in the evening is 6 pm.

On a 24-hour clock, times after midday are shown with numbers above 12. You can work out that 17:30 is 5:30 pm by subtracting 12 from the hour number.
See also **calendar, day, month, week, year.**

ton

A ton is a measure of mass or weight in the **imperial system**. A ton is 2240 pounds. A large car weighs about one ton. It is slightly heavier than a **tonne**.

tonne (t)

A tonne is a measure of mass or weight in the **metric system**. A tonne is 1000 kilograms (kg). A tonne weighs just less than a ton in the **imperial system**.

torus

A torus is a solid ring or doughnut shape with a hole in the middle.
See also **shape.**

total

The total is the result when you add together a group of numbers. A supermarket till works out the total you must pay for your shopping by adding together the price of everything in your basket or trolley.
See also **addition, sum.**

transform

Transform means to change. When you hold your hand in front of a mirror, the reflection transforms your left hand into a right hand. If you add 1 to an even number it transforms into an odd number.
See also **function, reflection.**

translation

A translation is a movement of a shape in a straight line. You can make a regular pattern of potato prints by repeating the same translations again and again.
See also **symmetry.**

trapezium

A trapezium is a flat, or plane, shape with four sides. Two sides are **parallel** and two are not parallel. In the United States, this shape is called a trapezoid.

> *Be careful not to get confused when you discuss these shapes with someone from the USA!*

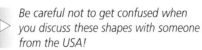

trapezium (UK)

trapezoid (USA)

trapezium (USA)

trapezoid (UK)

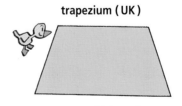

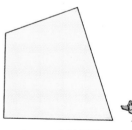

trapezoid

A trapezoid is a flat, or plane, shape with four sides. None of the sides are **parallel**. In the USA this is called a trapezium.

triangle

A triangle is a flat, or plane, shape with three sides. The three angles of a triangle always add up to 180 degrees (180°).

See also **equilateral triangle, isosceles triangle, right-angled triangle.**

equilateral

right-angled

scalene (no equal sides)

isosceles

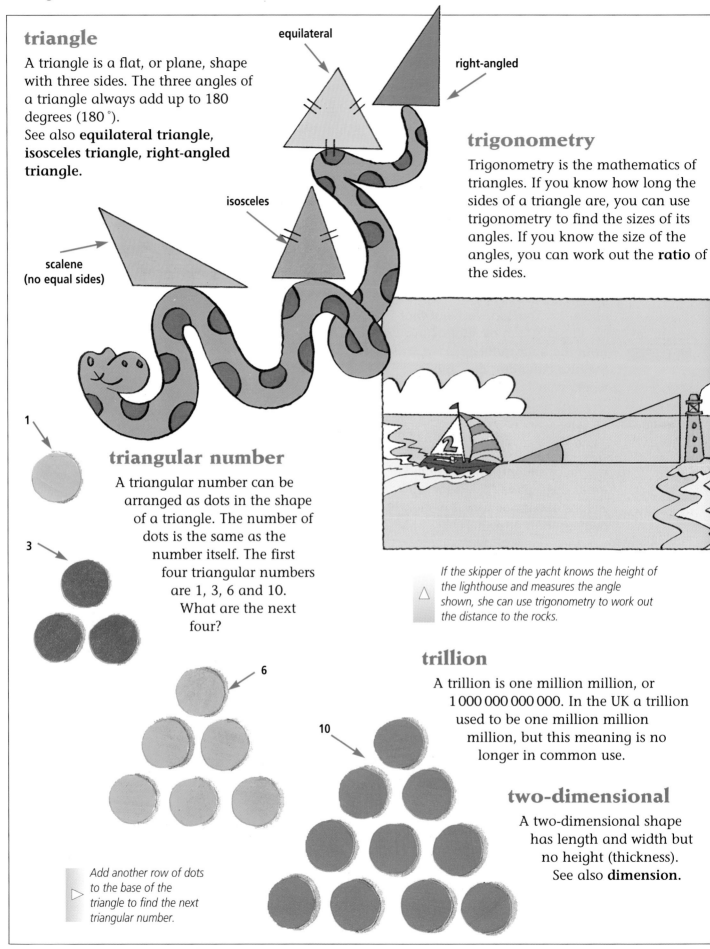

trigonometry

Trigonometry is the mathematics of triangles. If you know how long the sides of a triangle are, you can use trigonometry to find the sizes of its angles. If you know the size of the angles, you can work out the **ratio** of the sides.

triangular number

A triangular number can be arranged as dots in the shape of a triangle. The number of dots is the same as the number itself. The first four triangular numbers are 1, 3, 6 and 10. What are the next four?

1

3

6

10

If the skipper of the yacht knows the height of the lighthouse and measures the angle shown, she can use trigonometry to work out the distance to the rocks.

trillion

A trillion is one million million, or 1 000 000 000 000. In the UK a trillion used to be one million million million, but this meaning is no longer in common use.

two-dimensional

A two-dimensional shape has length and width but no height (thickness). See also **dimension.**

Add another row of dots to the base of the triangle to find the next triangular number.

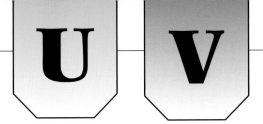

unit

A unit is one thing or object. The units column in a number tells you how many ones, or units, there are between 0 and 9 in that number. In the number 357, the digit 7 tells you that the number has seven ones, or units.

A unit is also an amount of something. We measure length, time, weight and other quantities in special units. We measure how long something is in units called metres (m). See also **decimal number, measure.**

Venn diagram

A Venn diagram is a drawing to show how different things can be sorted into groups. The groups are known as **sets**. A line surrounds everything in the same set.

In some places the sets in a Venn diagram overlap or intersect. Things that belong to two or more different sets at once are placed in these intersections.
See also **Carroll diagram.**

Because red triangles are both triangles and red shapes, they are in both sets at once in this Venn diagram. Things that are neither triangles nor red shapes are outside both sets.

This stained-glass window shows a Venn diagram for three overlapping sets.

vertex

A vertex is one of the corners of a triangle, a square, a **polygon**, or a solid shape. Two or more lines meet at a vertex to make an angle.

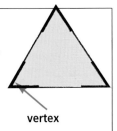

vertex

vertical

A vertical line is at right angles to flat, or **horizontal**, ground. A builder uses a plumb bob to check that a wall is vertical. A plumb bob is a heavy weight on a string. The force of **gravity** pulls the weight towards the centre of the Earth. This force makes the string hang down vertically.

volume

vertical line

volume

The volume of an object is the amount of space it fills. You can use special **formulas** to work out the volume of a solid with a regular shape, such as a **cube**. To find the volume of a cube, you multiply its length by its width by its height.

The volume of a cube with 1-metre sides is 1 cubic metre (1 m x 1 m x 1 m). The volume of a 2-metre cube is 8 cubic metres (2 m x 2 m x 2 m). What is the volume of a 3-metre cube?

You can find the volume of a solid with an irregular shape by putting it into a measuring-jug of water. Push the solid under the water's surface and measure the amount that the water rises on the jug's scale. The volume of the water pushed aside, or displaced, is the same as the volume of the irregular solid.
See also **capacity.**

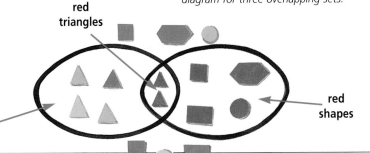

red triangles

triangles

red shapes

63

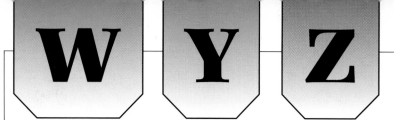

W Y Z

week

There are seven days in one week. A year has 52 weeks and one day (or two days in a leap year). The extra day in each year means that if your birthday is on a Monday this year, it will be on a Tuesday next year. (If the extra day of a leap year, 29 February, comes before your next birthday then your birthday will be on a Wednesday next year.)
See also **calendar, month, time.**

▷ The Earth takes just one year to complete its orbit of the Sun.

weight

How much do you weigh?
A force called **gravity** pulls on your body and gives you weight. It also keeps you on the ground. We usually measure weight in kilograms (kg), which are really units for measuring **mass**.

whole number

Whole numbers are 1, 2, 3 and so on. They have no parts that are fractions. Whole numbers can be positive or negative. Another name for a whole number is an **integer**.
See also **number.**

yard (yd)

A yard is a measure of length in the **imperial system**. There are three feet in one yard. It is about the length of a long stride by an adult.
See also **measure.**

year

A year is the time that the Earth takes to travel all the way around the Sun in its orbit. In one year the Earth turns on its own **axis** $365\frac{1}{4}$, times. To make things easy, we say that there are 365 days in a year, but we add together the four $\frac{1}{4}$ days to make an extra day in the calendar every fourth year. This extra day is 29 February.
See also **calendar, time.**

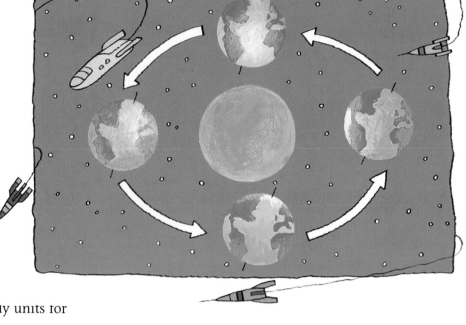

zero

Zero is the symbol for nothing or **nought**. It is written as 0. The Romans had no symbol for zero, so their numbers were complicated to use. They had to write separate letters for units, tens, hundreds and thousands. If we want to change a number from a unit to a ten, a hundred or a thousand, we just add a zero each time: 2, 20, 200, 2000.

 Did you know?
A number plus zero = the number
A number minus zero = the number
A number times zero = zero
A number divided by zero = infinity.